Richard Newton

The giants and how to fight them

Richard Newton

The giants and how to fight them

ISBN/EAN: 9783337135782

Printed in Europe, USA, Canada, Australia, Japan

Cover: Foto ©Lupo / pixelio.de

More available books at **www.hansebooks.com**

THE GIANTS,

AND

HOW TO FIGHT THEM;

AND

Wonderful Things

BY THE

REV. RICHARD NEWTON, D.D.

NEW YORK:
ROBERT CARTER & BROTHERS,
530 Broadway.
1875.

CONTENTS.

	PAGE
THE GIANTS	7
THE FIRST GIANT	18
THE SECOND GIANT	32
THE THIRD GIANT	44
THE FOURTH GIANT	60
THE FIFTH GIANT	71

WONDERFUL THINGS.

I. THE WONDERFUL STAFF	199
II. THE WONDERFUL COMFORTER	244
III. THE WONDERFUL GUIDE	287

THE GIANTS.

"So David prevailed over the Philistine with a sling and with a stone, and smote the Philistine, and slew him."—1. SAM. xvii. 50.

THE Philistine spoken of here, was the giant Goliath. Now let us put the word Giant instead of the Philistine, and then the text will read in this way:—"So David prevailed over the giant with a sling and a stone, and smote the giant, and slew him." All young people like to hear, and read stories about giants. I suppose there is hardly a person in this country who knows how to read but who has read the famous history of "Jack the Giant Killer." I remember, when a very little boy, reading it, and thinking what a wonderful history it was. I need not tell you, however, that that history has not a word of truth in it. No such person as the celebrated "Jack" ever lived. And the giants, he is said to have killed so nimbly, never lived either.

But the verse we have taken

for our text to-day, tells us about David the Giant Killer. He was a real person. He actually lived, about 3000 years ago. And the giant, whom he killed, was a real live giant. He was a pretty big fellow too, though not so enormously large as some of the story books would lead us to think. Such huge monsters as they represent, never existed anywhere, except in the thoughts of those who write books of fables, and stories that are not true. Goliath, the giant whom David killed, was six cubits and a span in height.

There are different opinions about the size of the Jewish measure called a cubit. One of these opinions is that it was twenty-one inches, and about two-thirds of an inch. At this rate, six cubits would be about eleven feet four inches. A span is six inches. This added to the other would give us eleven feet ten inches as Goliath's height. Now take two men, each of whom is five feet eleven inches high; let one of them stand upon the head of the other, making as it were, one man; and suppose him to be stout and strong in proportion to his height, and then you would have a man of about Goliath's size. The coat of mail that he wore, weighed about 150 pounds. His armor altogether, weighed about 272. That is nearly as much as five fifty-six pound weights. The armor of an ordinary soldier in those times, weighed about 60 pounds. How frightful it must have been to see this vast creature, with all his armor on, and his huge spear in his hand, stalk forth before all the army of the Israelites, and dare any one of them to come out, and fight with him! We do not wonder that all the soldiers fled away at his approach, and that no one was willing to go and fight him. And we admire very much the courage of David, and his confidence in God, that he, a mere shepherd's boy, was willing, with nothing in his hand but a sling and a stone, to go and do battle with this great giant. You know how angry the giant was when he saw this beardless boy come against him; and what dreadful things he threatened to do to David; and how David ran and took a stone, and slung it; and how it went whizzing along, till it hit him in the forehead, and he fell senseless to the ground.

Some people pretend to think that it was hardly possible for David to throw a stone with sufficient force to sink into the giant's head. One of this class, a foolish young man, who pretended not to believe the Bible, was once riding in a stage-coach, which was full of passengers. He was trying to ridicule some of the Bible stories. Among others, he spoke of this one about David, and the giant. He said he thought the giant's head must have been too hard for a boy, like David, to send a stone into it; and turning to an old Quaker gentleman, who sat in the corner of the coach, he asked, "What do you think about it, sir?"

"Friend," said the old gentleman, in a dry, quiet way, "I'll tell thee what I think; if the giant's head was as soft as thine, it must have been very easy for the stone to get in."

But David DID kill the giant. Yes, and we read about several of the giant's brothers who were killed in David's time. The whole family of them was destroyed. But the giants are not all dead yet. There ARE giants in the earth in these days. And God expects us all to engage in the work of trying to fight them. When I speak of giants, now, I do not mean physical giants, but moral giants. I do not mean men with huge bodies, four or five times larger than common sized men; but I mean great sins of different kinds, which may well be called giants.

I want now to speak about five giants that we should all unite in trying to fight against. One of these is a good way off from us; but the rest are very near us. Listen to me, while I tell you who these giants are, and the way in which we must try to fight them.

The First Giant.

The first giant I am to speak of, is the Giant Heathenism.

This giant doesn't live here. He is found in countries where the Gospel is not known. His castles may be seen in Africa, and in India, in China, and in the islands of the sea. He is a huge giant. He has a great many heads, more indeed than I can pretend to count. In every country where idols are worshipped one of the heads of this giant may be found. One of these heads is called Juggernaut; another is called Brahma; another Buddha, and many such like names. This giant is very strong, and very cruel. We read, in that interesting book called "Pilgrim's Progress," about a giant whose name was Despair, and who lived in a castle called "Doubting Castle." He used to seize the pilgrims to the heavenly city, as they ventured on his grounds. When he had caught them, he used to thrust them into a dark, dismal dungeon, and beat them with his great club;—and treat them so badly that many of them were driven to kill themselves. He was a very strong giant, and very cruel. And Heathenism, the giant of whom I am speaking, is just like him, in these respects.

HE IS VERY STRONG. He is so strong that he keeps six hundred millions of people in his dungeons all the time. They are bound hand and foot. They can not possibly get out, till the friends of Jesus attack the giant, and make him let go of them.

And he is VERY CRUEL, as well as very strong. The things that are done in some of the dungeons where he dwells, show how cruel he is. Look at India. There is Juggernaut, one of the heads of this giant. This idol is kept on a great heavy car. At certain seasons of the year, when they have a festival, this car is dragged out. Hundreds of people take hold of the rope and pull it along;— and while it rolls on, great numbers of men and women will throw themselves down, before the car, and be crushed to death under its wheels, as they roll over them. For miles, around the temple, you may see the bones of the poor creatures who have been crushed in this way.

In other parts of his dungeon, this giant makes his poor wretched prisoners put iron hooks through the flesh, on the back of their bodies—and then swing themselves round, with the whole weight of their bodies resting on these hooks.

In other parts, he makes his poor prisoners kill a great many of their little innocent children, as soon as they are born. Sometimes their parents will dig a hole in the ground, and bury their baby, alive, in it. Sometimes they will throw them into the river, to be drowned, or devoured by alligators. In some places, along the river Ganges, there are crocodiles that live almost altogether on the dear little babies that are thrown in, by their cruel mothers, to be devoured alive, by those horrible monsters.

In the South Sea Islands, three out of four, of all the children born, used to be killed.

In one tribe of people in India that numbered 12,000 men — there were only thirty women. All the rest had been killed when they were young.

In the city of Pekin many infants are thrown out into the streets, every night. Sometimes they are killed, at once, by the fall. Sometimes they are only half killed, and linger, moaning in agony, till the morning. Then the police go round, and pick them up, and throw them, altogether, into a hole, and bury them.

In Africa, the children are sometimes burnt alive. In India, they are sometimes exposed in the woods till they either starve to death, or are devoured by the jackals, and vultures. In the South Sea Islands they used, sometimes, to strangle their babies;

while at other times they would break all their joints, first their fingers and toes, then their ankles and wrists, and then their elbows and knees.

Surely they are horrible dungeons in which such dreadful things are done!

And the giant Heathenism, who makes his prisoners do such things, must be indeed a cruel giant!

Well, what are we to do to this giant? Why, we must FIGHT him, as David did Goliath. We do not expect to kill him outright. He will never be killed till Jesus comes again. He Himself will kill the giant Heathenism. But we can cut off some of the giants' heads, and set some of his prisoners free. We are bound, in duty, to fight against this giant. But how are we to do this? Just as David did. He fought against Goliath with a sling and a stone. He picked the stones out of the brook, and hurled them at the giant. And this is what we must do. The Bible is the brook to which we must go. The truths which it contains are the stones that we must use. When these truths are hurled against the head of this giant, they will sink into it just as David's pebble did into Goliath's head—and he will fall.

A Chinese idolater had become a Christian. He stood among his countrymen, one day, distributing some tracts. They were taken into the interior of China, and read. The reading of them led the people of many towns and villages to give up the worship of idols. This destroyed one of the heads of the giant. In the Sandwich Islands another of his heads has been destroyed;—and another in the Islands of New Zealand:—and another in the Feejee Islands. And Sunday-school children are trying to help in this work, when they assist in making contributions to the missionary cause. We are helping to throw the stones of truth at the heads of the giant Heathenism. When the Missionaries preach of

Jesus to the heathen, they are slinging stones at the giant's head. God directs the stones which they throw, and makes them effectual to wound, and disable the giant. David never could have killed Goliath, if left to himself. But God helped him, and then the stone did its work. And so God will help us: so He will help all who fight against the great cruel giant — Heathenism. Then let us go on, like brave giant-killers, and fight against this giant. We are sure to succeed—for God has promised that the giant shall be killed at last.

The first giant is HEATHENISM: and we are to fight against him by throwing stones of truth at him.

But now let us go on to speak of some other giants. The one I have just spoken of lives a great way off from us. The others we are to fight against, live near us. They may be found in our own country;—in our own city;— in our own homes;— yes, and even in our OWN HEARTS.

The Second Giant.

The second giant I would speak of, is the Giant Selfishness.

Now, remember, I am not speaking of physical giants, but moral giants; — not of giants made of flesh and blood, but of giants made of thoughts and feelings. This giant Selfishness is an intensely ugly looking creature. If he could be caught, in a bodily shape, and carried to some daguerreotype office to have his likeness taken, I am sure that, when you came to look at his picture, you would think it about the ugliest you had ever seen.

How many eyes have you? Two. How many ears? Two. How many hands? Two. And how many feet? Two. Yes, God has given us each two eyes, two ears, two hands, and two feet, as if it were to remind us that we are to see, and hear, and work, and walk, for others, as well as for ourselves. But how many mouths have you? One. Yes, for we have to eat for ourselves only, and not for others. But the giant Selfishness never sees, or hears, or does anything for any one but himself. If we had a correct likeness of him, we should see a huge one-eyed, one-eared, one-armed monster, with his other eye, and ear, and arm shrivelled, and dried up like a mummy's, for want of use. The business of this giant is to take people prisoners, and drag them to his castle. If they stay there long they begin to grow just like him, ugly, one-sided looking creatures. I do not mean to say, that this change takes place in their bodies, but it does in their souls. They learn to love none but themselves. They think and care for none but themselves. This giant is trying all the time to bind his chains on people, and make them his prisoners. He likes especially to do this while they are young.

But if he does not appear in a

bodily form, how may we know when he is trying to fasten his chains on us and make us his prisoners?

Let me tell you. If you find that you are getting to think more of YOURSELF, than of others, then be sure the giant is after you. If you see a boy, or girl, enter a room, and go and take the best seat in it, when older persons are present; if you see them pick out for themselves the largest piece of cake, or the biggest and nicest apple, when these

THE SECOND GIANT.

are handed round, you may be sure the giant Selfishness is at work on them. He is fastening his chains upon them; and if they don't take care, he will soon have them as his prisoners.

Now, we must ALL FIGHT this giant. But HOW are we to do this? Not by standing off at a distance, and throwing stones at him, as we are to do with the giant Heathenism. This will not do here. No, THIS must be a close, hand-to-hand fight. We must grapple him, and wrestle with him. WE MUST FIGHT THIS GIANT BY SELF-DENIAL.

Let me show you what I mean by this. There were two little boys, named James and William. One day, as they were just starting for school, their father gave them each a three-cent piece to spend for themselves. The little fellows were very much pleased with this, and went off, as merry as crickets.

"What are you going to buy, William?" said James, after they had walked a little way.

"I don't know," William replied, "I have not thought yet. What are you going to buy?"

"Why, I tell you what I believe I'll do. You know mother is sick. Now, I think I'll buy her a nice orange. I think it will taste good to her."

"You may do so, if you please, James," said William; "but I'm going to buy something for MYSELF. Father gave me the money to spend for myself, and I mean to do it. If mother wants an orange, she can send for it. She's got money, and Hannah gets every thing she wants."

"I know that," said James, "but then it would make me feel so happy to see her eating an orange that I had bought for her with my own money. She is always doing something for us, or getting us some nice thing, and I want to let her see that I don't forget it."

"Do as you please," said William, "but I go in for the candy."

Presently they came to the confectioner's shop. William invested his three cents in cream-candy;—but James bought a nice orange. When they went home at noon, he went into his mother's chamber, and said: "See, Ma', what a nice orange I have brought you!"

"It is, indeed, very nice, my son, and it will taste very good to me. I have been wanting an orange all the morning. Where did you get it?"

"Pa' gave me three cents this morning, and I bought it with them."

"You are very good, my dear boy, to think of your sick mother. And you wouldn't spend your money for cakes, or candy, but denied yourself, that you might get an orange for me. Mother loves you for this exercise of self-denial." And then she threw her arms around his neck, and kissed him.

Now, here, you see how the giant Selfishness made an attack on these two boys. James fought him off, bravely, by the EXERCISE OF SELF-DENIAL. William refused to exercise self-denial, and so the giant got a hitch of his chain around him. We shall find this giant making attacks upon us all the time. We can only fight him off by SELF-DENIAL.

The Third Giant.

The third giant I want to speak about, is the Giant Covetousness.

This giant is very large in size, and very strong in limb; but he has the tiniest little bit of a heart you ever saw. It isn't bigger than a Bantam chicken's heart. You might put it in a nutshell. The only wonder is, how so huge a frame can be supported by so

little a heart. But this is not all,
for little as his heart is, it is as hard
as stone. We sometimes hear of
people dying with what is called
the OSSIFICATION of the heart.
Ossification means, turning to
bone. When a man's heart gets
hard, or turns to bone, he dies.
According to this rule the giant
Covetousness ought to have been
dead long ago. It's a perfect
wonder how he manages to live,
with his little heart all turned to
stone. But he DOES live; yes,
and not only lives, but is hearty

and strong. He is very active. His castle is of great size, and he always has it crowded with prisoners. Those whom he once fairly gets into his chains, find it very hard to break loose. Yet this is very strange, for he is a most disagreeable creature. He drives the poor away from his door. If a shivering beggar comes by, he buttons up his pocket, lest by any means a penny should happen to get out. He can hear about poor widows and orphans starving with hunger, and perishing with cold, but never sheds a tear, or heaves a sigh, or gives the least trifle for their relief. When he knows of worthy people being in need, he "shutteth up his compassion from them." His heart is hard as a rock, and cold as an iceberg. He loves money better than any thing else in the world. He gets all he can, and keeps all he gets. He is ashamed of his name, and won't answer to it. He pretends that his right name is — FRUGALITY. But this is a great story. Frugality is a very different person. He is a good, true, honest fellow. I know he is a sort of SECOND COUSIN of the giants, and some people think he looks very much like him; but I don't think he does at all. At any rate this is NOT the giant's name. His own, real, proper name is COVETOUSNESS; and his puny, little, stony heart PROVES it.

Well, his prisoners all become wonderfully like him. Their hearts shrivel up till they are almost as little, and as hard as his. But how may we know when he is trying to make people his prisoners? Very easily. When you see people learning to love their money more than they used to do;— when they always tie their purse-strings very tight, and are very slow to untie them;—when you hear them, all the time, grumbling about there being so many collections taken up, — and so many calls for money;—when you find them unwilling to give; —when you see them wince and wriggle under parting with a little money, as though you were drawing one of their eye-teeth out of their heads, then you may know that the giant Covetousness has got a hold upon these people.

My dear children, I want you all to fight bravely against this giant. If you ask, How are you to fight him? I answer, By LEARNING TO GIVE. He hates giving, above all things. It hurts his feelings dreadfully. Once get into the habit of giving, and he never can fasten his chains upon you.

"Mother," asked a little boy

who was trying to make a good beginning of the new year, "How much of my spending money do you think I ought to give to God?"

"I don't know," said his mother — "How much have you?" He opened his wallet, and out dropped, on the table, a gold dollar his grandmother had given him for a Christmas present, a five-cent piece, and a three-cent piece.

"There's my gold dollar,—I'll halve that," said he; "five cents and three cents are eight cents, and half of that is four. But, no. I'll give the largest half to God. I'll give Him half the dollar, and the five cents."

I don't believe the giant Covetousness will ever get a single link of his chain fastened on the limbs of that noble-hearted boy.

But I want to tell you about a great battle, once fought, between this giant and a Deacon, in a church in New England. We may call the Deacon's name, Holdfast. The story is a true one, though this was not the man's real name. Before Deacon Holdfast became a Christian, he had been a prisoner of the giant's for years. The chains of the giant had been so riveted, upon his limbs, that he found it very hard to get rid of them. Many a sharp conflict they had together. Sometimes the Deacon would get the victory, but more frequently the giant. Still the Deacon wouldn't give up. He was determined not to wear the giant's chain. And after the fight that I'm going to tell you about, he got such an advantage over the giant that he never troubled him much again. It happened in this way.

In the same church, to which the Deacon belonged, there was a worthy, honest, good man, who was very poor. This poor man had the misfortune to lose his cow. She died. The poor man was in great distress. The cow was his chief dependence for the support of his family. He went and told the Deacon about his trouble. In order to aid him in getting another cow, the good Deacon drew up a subscription-paper, and put his own name down, at the head of it, for five dollars, which he paid over. This made the giant Covetousness very angry. He took on dreadfully. He began to rave and storm, and tried to frighten the Deacon.

"What's the use of all this waste?" he cried. "Charity begins at home. The more you give, the more you may give. Why can't you let people take care of themselves? What right have you to take the bread out of the mouths of your own children, and give it to strangers? Go on at this rate, and the poorhouse, wretchedness, poverty, and rags, are what you will come to."

This made the Deacon angry. His spirit was roused. He went to the poor man to whom he had given the subscription, and told him he must give him back the five dollars. The poor fellow's heart sunk within him. He thought he should never get his cow again. But he handed over the money. The Deacon stood a moment as if hesitating what to do. At last he said to the poor man;—" My brother, some people are very much troubled with their old women, but I am troubled most with my OLD MAN. He has been scolding me dreadfully for giving you so much money; but now I mean to fix him." And then turning round, as if addressing the giant, he said;—" Old fellow, I want you to understand that I mean to give away just as much money as I think right." And then opening his wallet, and taking out a ten dollar bill, he added,—" I shall now give this good brother ten dollars instead of five, and if you say another word I'll give him TWENTY, instead of ten!"

This was a dreadful blow to the giant. It laid him sprawling on the ground. It took him, as the Bible says, " under the fifth rib." It knocked the breath clean out of him. He hadn't a word to say.

LEARNING TO GIVE is the way in which to fight the giant Covetousness.

The Fourth Giant.

THE fourth giant of which I will speak, is the GIANT ILL-TEMPER.

This giant is not so large, or strong as the others, but he is quite as ugly. He is found in more places than the last. He has more to do with young people than either of the others, though he does attack old people too, sometimes. He is always in a pet. From constant pouting, his lips have grown horribly thick and ugly-looking. He is frowning all the time, till his forehead is as full of wrinkles, and as rough as the bark of an old oak tree. Sometimes his eyes are red with weeping, and at other times they are all in a flame with anger. Sometimes his voice bellows like thunder; and then again it will resemble the low hoarse growl of a surly dog.

He may generally be found hanging round the nursery, the

dining or sitting-room, ready to pounce upon the children, and make them prisoners. And, when he gets hold of them, he makes them so ugly and disagreeable that no one cares to have any thing to do with them.

Now let me give you some signs by which you may know when this giant is getting hold of a boy or girl. He generally waits and watches till he hears them asked to do something which he knows they don't like. Then he is ready, in a moment, to begin his attack. He makes the eye begin to frown. He puckers up the mouth; he makes the lips pout, and swell out to twice their usual size. The fingers begin to wriggle about, like a set of worms; or, sometimes, one of the fingers goes into the corner of the mouth. The shoulders are seen to twist about, first one way, and then another. If the boy has a book in his hand, down it drops on the floor; or, else, it is flung across the room. If he is walking, he stamps, with his foot, as if he were trying to get a tight shoe on. If he is sitting, his feet begin to swing, backwards and forwards, and make a great noise, by striking against the chair. Sometimes he seems to become deaf and dumb. He hears nothing, — and says nothing. At other times he speaks, but it is just like a dog when snarling over a bone.

Whenever you see these signs, you may know that this ugly giant is about, and is busy making prisoners. And if you don't fight bravely against him, he will fasten his chains on you, and then you will be spoiled.

BUT HOW ARE WE TO FIGHT AGAINST THIS GIANT? I answer;—BY TRYING TO BE LIKE JESUS.

We always think of Him as—the "gentle Jesus, meek and mild." Do you suppose that this giant ever got a single link of his chain on Jesus? No. Do you suppose Jesus ever spoke a cross word to any one? No. Do you suppose He ever did an unkind act to any one? No. We have no particular history of the childhood of Jesus. But we know how He acted when He was a man;— and we know that He was always the same. If we try to be like Jesus, the giant Illtemper will never get hold of us. When you are tempted to speak cross words, or to do unkind things, ask yourself the question, What would Jesus do, or say, if He were in my situation? In this way you will always be able to fight off this giant.

I was reading lately about two

little sisters, who always lived happily together. The giant Ill-temper never could catch them. They had the same books and the same playthings, yet they never quarrelled. No cross words, no pouts, no slaps, no running away in a pet, ever took place with them. Whether they were sitting on the green before the door, or playing with their old dog, Congo, or dressing their dolls, or helping their mother, they were always the same sweet-tempered little girls.

"You never seem to quarrel," said a lady, visiting at their house, one day. "How is it that you are always so happy together?"

They looked up, and the eldest answered;—"I 'spose it's 'cause Addie lets me, and i let Addie."

Ah! yes, it's just this letting that keeps the giant off. What a beautiful picture that is of those sweet-tempered sisters! But see what a different one this is.

A mother hears a noise under the window. She looks out.

"Gerty, what's the matter?"

"Mary won't let me have her ball," cries Gerty.

"Well, Gerty wouldn't let me have her pencil in school," cries Mary, "and I don't mean she shall have my ball."

"Fie, fie, is that the way for sisters to act towards each other?" says the mother.

"She'll only lose my pencil," mutters Gerty, "and she sha'n't have it."

"And she'll only lose my ball," replies Mary, "and I won't let her have it!"

Ah, the giant had got fast hold of these two girls. They didn't know how to fight him. They were not trying to be like Jesus.

The Fifth Giant.

The last giant I wish to speak about, is the Giant Intemperance.

When a person is making a speech, and giving reasons to persuade those who hear him to do anything, he generally keeps the strongest reason for the last. And so I have put the giant Intemperance last, and shall say more about him than any of the others, because he is the most important. He is the worst giant of the whole lot, as I think you will be ready to own after you have heard a little about him.

He is a very ugly looking fellow. When he is in a good humor, and feels jolly, he puts on a silly face, and looks very foolish. But when he gets in a passion, he is awful looking, and it makes one shudder to see him. He never was very handsome, even when he was quite young; but as he has grown older, and more

wicked, evil passions have shown themselves more and more on his countenance, and sin has stamped its dreadful mark upon his features so fearfully, that he is now a very monster of ugliness. And he is so filthy, too, that his whole appearance is disgusting. Generally he is clothed in rags. Often he is seen covered with dirt, gathered from the gutter where he has been lying. His face is frequently all bruised and swollen, from the fights in which he has been engaging. Sometimes he goes unwashed and unshaved for days together; and then, with a rough, shaggy beard, and with an old crumpled hat on his head, he may be seen reeling and staggering about the streets, a perfect nuisance to the neighborhood.

He is very wicked, too. He breaks every commandment of God's law. He is the author of nearly every crime that is committed. It is he who sets on men and women to sin. He fills our almshouses, our prisons, and penitentiaries. If it were not for him, we might dismiss most of our police, do without half our courts, close our station-houses, tear down our prisons, and burn our gallows. Sin follows him like a shadow, wherever he goes. Quarrelling, swearing, fighting, robbing, murdering, and all kinds of wickedness abound where this giant dwells.

Of all the giants in this country he is the largest, the most powerful, and in every way the most dangerous. He is stronger here than almost any where else.

There was a time when he might easily have been driven out of the land. But now he has built so many castles, and gloomy dungeons; he has so many thousands of men in his service, and so much money to use in his defence, that he bids defiance to his enemies. More sermons and speeches have been delivered against him, more books written, more societies formed, and more efforts made in every way against him, than all the rest put together.

And though he is thousands

of years old, and has been through hundreds of battles, he does not seem to grow weak, or stiff with age, like giant Paganism, that Bunyan tells of in the "Pilgrim's Progress." But every year he seems to get stronger and more active. And oh! what a sad sight it is to look into his dungeons! Hundreds, and thousands of prisoners, in our land, are bound fast in his chains. He has more of them than any other giant here. And they are not from any one class only The rich and the poor, the high and the low, are among them. Laboring men, mechanics, merchants, lawyers, doctors, ministers; men and women, and even children too, are dragged into his dungeons. The most accomplished, the most talented, the most beautiful, the most amiable, fall under his power. Thirty thousand captives are taken from his dungeons, in our own country, every year, and buried in the drunkard's grave. How dreadful this is to think of!

We read in history, that a good

many years ago, when Greece was one of the first nations of the world, there was a great monster who troubled a part of that land very much. He made them send him, every year, seven boys and seven girls. These he used to eat. And every year, when the time came for sending these poor children, what a scene of sorrow there was! How the parents cried, and how the friends and relatives cried! And how those who were going to be slaughtered cried, as they went on board the great ship, with black sails, that carried the victims to the monster! Those people thought it was a terrible thing to have that dreadful plague devour FOURTEEN of their children every year. But what was that Grecian monster, in comparison with this awful giant Intemperance? He takes THIRTY THOUSAND men, and women, and children, every year, and devours them.

Of course, he must be very busy making prisoners, to be able to take so many. He sets a great many traps, and snares, to catch people. The taverns, grog-shops, lager-beer houses, and drinking saloons, along our streets, are all TRAPS he has set. There he sits, watching to catch any passer-by, just as you often see a spider quietly waiting in its web to entangle some poor fly. Into these traps people are enticed. They are tempted to drink. They learn to love drinking. And when this habit is formed, they become his prisoners. But these are not his only snares. He is very cunning, and often catches people where they have no idea there is any danger.

Sometimes he puts little traps inside of tempting looking sugar-plums, to catch boys and girls. He drops a little wine, or cordial, or brandy, into these sugar-plums, and then spreads them out in the store windows. These are bought, and eaten. The taste for liquor is formed, and so by degrees the giant fastens his chain upon the buyers, till they, too, become his prisoners.

Sometimes he spreads a snare in the social evening party. A pleasant company is assembled. Refreshments are handed round. Wine is poured out. A young man is asked to take some, but declines. He is pressed to drink to the health of a friend. He hesitates, not wishing to hurt his friend's feelings, but thinks he can't refuse without doing so. The sparkling glass is taken. Then another, and another, till at last he is intoxicated. The giant has fastened the first link of his cruel chain upon him. The taste for drink is formed now. He wants more and more. By and by he can't do without it. The giant has bound him, hand and foot, and he is dragged helplessly down to ruin.

These are some of his ways of catching people. He does not pounce upon them, and drag them off at once; but he captures them by degrees. Do you know how a boa-constrictor seizes a sheep, or a cow? When he sees one coming, he darts suddenly forth, throws a part of his huge body around the animal, then another, and another, till he has bound it so tight that it can not move. It is unable to resist then, and the serpent crushes it to death in his powerful folds. Well, just so this giant fights. He does not bind his prisoners fast, at once, but winds himself gradually about them. Every time they drink liquor, he throws a fold around them. Tighter and tighter he grasps them, until he has them completely in his power. When you see a person beginning to drink intoxicating liquor of any kind, be sure the giant is after him. You may always know when he is coming, and I will tell you how. Did you ever see a shark? You know what horrible creatures they are, and how much the sailors dread them. They will bite off a man's leg, or even swallow him whole, and make nothing of it. Well, you can always tell when a shark is about. He sends a little fish ahead of him, called the pilot-fish. If you see one of these about the vessel, then look out for a shark. He is certainly near, and you will soon see him. Now, the giant Intemperance always sends a sort of pilot-fish ahead of him. He never comes before it; but is pretty sure to come after it. Wherever you see it, look out for the giant. Do you know what it is? It is A BOTTLE, or DECANTER. When you see one of these in use, you may be sure the giant is not far off.

When a person gets into his

power, every thing begins to go wrong with him. His business is neglected. His money is squandered. He becomes unkind to his wife and children, or undutiful to his parents. He spends for drink, that which should go to support his family. He becomes cruel, and hard-hearted, passionate, and fierce. His evil tempers are roused. They conquer his better feelings. He turns from the path of virtue, and enters that of vice. That is a down-hill path, and the giant pushes him on faster and faster. He loses all sense of shame, and hesitates not at any sin. There is nothing so mean, so base, so wicked, that the prisoner of this giant will not do. His prospects for the future are ruined, the moment he is securely bound. Yes, RUINED: ruined for time— and for eternity. Misery, poverty, disgrace, and want, are the portion the giant gives him while he lives; and, when he dies, he finds the truth of the Bible-statement, that "drunkards shall

NOT inherit the kingdom of God."

This giant Intemperance is the one we are now to speak about. Is he not a horrible fellow? And should we not all engage in fighting him?

Now, there are two things for us to consider:—How WE ARE TO FIGHT HIM; and WHY WE SHOULD FIGHT HIM. The way in which, and the reason why, we ought to fight him.

By fighting this giant Intemperance, I don't mean going into his dungeons, and trying to get his prisoners out. This we ought to do with all our hearts, whenever we can. But the kind of fighting I am going now to talk about is, what soldiers would call DEFENSIVE WARFARE,—that is, how to keep him off from OURSELVES, so that he shall not make us his prisoners.

We are to do this BY DRINKING COLD WATER. Of course, I do not mean to put cold water in opposition to milk, or tea, or coffee. If we only keep to such drinks as these, the giant's hands will never be laid on us. But I mean cold water in opposition to cider, beer, wine, brandy, gin, and the like, as our habitual drink.

Some people say, that it does no harm to drink A LITTLE. Let us see whether this is so or not.

Suppose you were on the top of a high mountain, and wanted to amuse yourself by rolling a large stone down its side. Some one, standing by, objects to this sport, telling you that it may perhaps fall on the head of a traveller, climbing up the mountain, and crush him to death; or break through the roof of some cottage, far down in the valley.

"Oh! no," you reply, "I only intend to roll it a LITTLE WAY. I don't mean to let it go far enough to do any mischief." But, if you bring it to the edge, and push it over, can you stop it when you please? Of course not. The easiest, the safest, the ONLY way to prevent any danger, would be, NOT TO SET IT IN MOTION AT ALL.

Just so it is with drinking. There is no danger while we keep to cold water, and let all kinds of liquor alone. But, if we begin taking a little now and then, we shall soon find it hard to stop; and, if the habit goes on increasing, it will, before long, be almost impossible to give it up. Every cup we take, like each successive roll of the stone, only makes the next more easy.

In the story of Sinbad, the sailor, we read that, in one of his voyages, he landed on a pleasant island. While walking about there, he met a little old man who asked him if he would not be so kind as to help him a little on his journey. Sinbad stooped down, picked him up, and set him on his shoulders. By and by he began to be tired, and wanted the old man to get down. But he wouldn't. After a little while, he asked him again to get off. But still he refused. Then Sinbad tried to shake him off. But he couldn't. The man clung on as if for life. So poor Sinbad had to journey on, and on, with this load upon his shoulders.

Now, if you let this giant once get hold of you,—you will have as much trouble to get rid of him as Sinbad had with the old man. He will probably cling to you, for life,—and be a load too heavy for you to bear. The only way is, to KEEP HIM OFF ALTOGETHER.

The great Dr. Johnson used to say, that it was easy not to drink at all, but hard to drink a little, and not soon take a great deal. There is danger in drinking liquor at all, but there is no danger in not drinking. One thing is certain; if we use only cold water, we shall never be made prisoners by this giant. He has no power at all over those who keep to cold water, and none of his attempts can succeed against them.

In Fairy tales we sometimes read about the CHARMS or TALISMANS, which the persons there described are said to wear. These are supposed to have the power of protecting those who use them, from all their enemies. No one, it was thought, could harm them while they had these about them. Well, COLD WATER is the talisman for us, — if we do not want to become prisoners of this giant. He never can conquer us while we make this our drink.

Now, the next thing we were to consider was, WHY we should fight against this giant.

There are FOUR reasons for doing so, in the way spoken of, that is, by the use of cold water.

The First Reason for Fighting.

We should fight against the giant in this way, because COLD WATER IS THE DRINK THAT GOD HAS MADE FOR US.

We have springs and fountains of water all over the world. They are found in every land. Wherever we find people living, there we find water for them to drink. But we never find any thing else than water in these springs.

Springs differ very much, both in taste and quality. The water from one spring will have sulphur in it;—another will have iron in it;—another will have magnesia in it;—another will have some kind of salt in it: but there never was a spring found in all the world that had alcohol in it. Alcohol, you know, is the part of wine or liquor that intoxicates, or makes people drunk. But alcohol is never found in the water that God has made, as it comes gushing up, pure and sparkling, from the earth. No body ever heard of a natural spring that yielded lager beer, or ale, or porter, or wine, or gin, or brandy. But if it had been good for us to have such drinks as these, God would have made them. He could have made springs that would yield different kinds of liquor just as easily as He made the trees to bear different kinds of fruit. If it had been necessary for us, there would have been, in every neighborhood, one or two beer, or ale, or brandy fountains. But you may travel round the globe, from East to West, from North to South;— you may visit every country, and examine every stream, and spring, and well; and you will not find any where a single beer, or wine, or brandy spring.

When God made Adam and Eve, you know He put them in the beautiful garden of Eden. In that garden, we are told, "the Lord God made to grow every tree that was pleasant to the sight and good for food. And a river went out of Eden to water the garden; and it was parted, and came into four heads." This is what the Bible tells us about that garden. We know it must have been very beautiful. Every thing that God makes is beautiful. When He makes a rainbow, how beautiful it is! When He makes a butterfly, how beautiful it is! When He makes a flower, a tree, a star, a sun, they are all beautiful. And when God undertook to make a garden, oh! how VERY beautiful it must have been!

What gently swelling hills!—what level plains!—what shady groves!—what velvet lawns!—what green, mossy banks!—what graceful trees!—what fragrant flowers!—what springs and fountains of cool, crystal water were there! Every thing that was pleasant to the eye and to the ear, to the taste and to the smell, was there; but do you suppose that in any part of the garden of Eden there was a wine or brandy fountain? No; nothing of the kind was found there.

Well, then, if cold water was the drink which God gave Adam in Eden; if cold water is the drink which God has made for us, and if it is the ONLY DRINK He has made for us, doesn't it follow very naturally that cold water is the best drink for us, and the one that we should use in preference to all others? And doesn't it follow, too, that we should have nothing to do with the giant Intemperance, but should resist him with all our might?

The first reason, then, why we

should fight against the giant Intemperance is, because COLD WATER IS THE DRINK GOD HAS MADE FOR US.

The Second Reason for Fighting.

We should fight against this Giant, because HE IS AN ENEMY TO HEALTH AND STRENGTH.

He never allows a prisoner of his to possess these blessings. He does not take them away at once; but, little by little, he robs every captive of them. The atmosphere of his dungeons is poisonous.

When one has been a captive of this giant for several years, what a picture of disease he presents! He is only the wreck of a man. His strength of body and of mind is gone; and his drooping head, his bloated face, his bloodshot eyes, his trembling hands, and staggering step, tell plainly what the giant has done for him. And then comes the delirium tremens, that dreadful sickness, caught only in this giant's dungeons, with all its horrors, and hurries the poor man off to the drunkard's grave.

And those whom the giant

only catches now and then, and who soon escape again from his clutches, do not get off uninjured. And even those who are never really made prisoners, who only take a little, do themselves harm. Many persons do not believe that this is so. They think a little wine, or brandy, strengthens them, and does them good, and that it is only because some people drink too much, and get intoxicated, that there is any harm done by drinking. But liquors will injure if taken at all, though the more we take the worse it will be for us.

Cold water, however, PROMOTES health and strength. There can be no doubt about this; neither can there be any doubt about the bad effect of liquors.

God is the wisest and most skilful physician in the universe. He knows what is best for the health and strength of people; and He prescribes cold water as the best drink.

Some years ago there was a man who had a severe wound in

his side. It healed at last, but left an opening, with a flap of skin lying over it, and through this opening persons could see right into his stomach. The physician who attended him, tried a great many interesting experiments upon him. When he made his patient drink cold water, and live on plain food, he found his stomach in a healthy state. When he made him use beer, or wine, or brandy, for several days, he found the inside of his stomach inflamed and sore;

and the man would complain of pain in his stomach, and headache, and say he felt very unwell.

There is an interesting story mentioned in the Bible that illustrates this point. You remember when Daniel and his companions went to Babylon, they were chosen, with a number of others, to go through a course of training to fit them for appearing in the presence of the king. While undergoing this training, they were expected to drink wine, and eat certain articles of food, which a pious Jew did not feel at liberty to use. The thought of doing this was a great trial to Daniel and his friends. They could not feel willing to do it. They, therefore, asked the officer who had charge of them, to excuse them from eating the meat and drinking the wine which the others used, and allow them to drink water and eat pulse, that is, such things as rice, beans, etc. The officer was a great friend to Daniel, and he said he would be very glad to accommodate him and his friends in this matter; but he was afraid that if he did so, they would grow thin and pale, while the rest would be looking hearty and strong; and then, when the king came to see them, he would be displeased at him, and perhaps order his head to be taken off. Then Daniel asked him to be so kind as to try the experiment for ten days, and see how it worked. He did so. Daniel and his friends had rice, and such like articles, for food,—and drank water;—while the other young men ate meat, and drank wine. At the end of ten days the officer found that Daniel and his companions were stouter and healthier than all the rest.

It is a great mistake to suppose that wine and liquors have the effect of making people strong and hearty. They have just the opposite effect. There is no drink that gives more real strength than cold water.

You know how strong the ox

and the horse are, and what hard work they have to do. Well, what do they drink? Water;—and nothing else. Take the horse, or the ox, after he has been ploughing hard all day, and is worn out with fatigue. Offer him a bucket of beer, or wine. Will he drink it? Not a drop. But give him a bucket of water, and how quickly he will drink it up. Water gives the horse his strength; and the ox, and the huge elephant, too.

Look at that giant oak tree.

How strong it is! Yet it drinks nothing but water. You know that trees DRINK, as well as men and cattle. The tree drinks through its roots, and through its leaves. If you break the tender stem of a plant or tree, you see a milky sort of liquid ooze out. We call it the sap. The sap is to the tree, just what the blood is to our bodies. Their growth and strength depend upon it. But water makes the best sap for the trees, as it makes the best blood for our bodies. Take any plant, and let it have nothing but wine, or beer, to moisten its leaves and roots, and it will die. Suppose it should rain wine or brandy for six months, what would the effect be? All the plants and trees would die.

One day a temperance man met a poor, miserable sailor, who had almost ruined himself with drink. He induced him to sign the pledge for one year. Jack liked the improvement in his health and prospects so much, that when the year was out, he went and renewed the pledge for ninety-nine years. He had just received his wages, which he was carrying in a bag in the inner side-pocket of his jacket. It looked like a great lump, or swelling, there. On his way home, he met the tavern-keeper, at whose house he used to spend his wages in liquor, and thought he would have a little fun with him.

"Well, old fellow," said the tavern-keeper, "how do you do?"

"Pretty well," said the sailor, "only I've got a hard lump here, on my side."

"Ah!" said the other, "it's cold water that has made that."

"Do you think so?"

"Yes, I know it. Only give up your miserable cold water slops, and drink some good liquor, and it will soon take the lump away."

"But," said the sailor, "I have just renewed the pledge, and I can't do it."

"Then mind what I say," said

the tavern-keeper,—" that lump will go on increasing, and very likely before another year you'll have one on the other side too."

"I hope I shall," said the sailor, taking out his bag of silver, and shaking it. "Good-bye."

Some years ago, a vessel, loaded with iron, was wrecked on the coast of New Jersey, in the winter-time. The hold of the vessel was partially filled with water. It was necessary to get the iron out before the vessel went to pieces. The weather was intensely cold, and to stand in the water and handle the cold iron, was very severe work. The men hired to unload the vessel, were divided into three sets, who were to relieve each other as often as might be necessary. The first set of men drank pretty freely of brandy, before they began, in order, as they said, to keep up their strength. They were worn out in about an hour. The next set drank hot coffee, and they stood the work for

above two hours. The third set were cold water men, and they were able to continue at the work for about three hours, before they were relieved.

A good many years ago, the crew of a Danish ship, numbering sixty persons, had to spend the winter up towards the North pole, in Hudson's Bay. They were supplied with provisions, and had plenty of liquor, of which they drank freely. Before spring FIFTY-EIGHT out of the sixty had died, leaving only two men to return home. Not long after, the crew of an English vessel, numbering twenty-two men, had to pass a winter in the same neighborhood. They had no ardent spirits with them, and only two of the company died during the whole winter.

When ships, on board of which much liquor is used, go into warm climates, they are always having sickness and death among the crews; but temperance ships will often make the same voyages, and hardly have a single case of sickness or death on board. This shows how health follows cold water drinkers, while it flies from the presence of the giant.

But nothing proves this more certainly, than to notice the different effect which disease has on those who are in the habit of drinking liquor, from what it has on those who drink water.

When a dreadful disease, like the cholera, or the yellow fever, breaks out, those who drink liquor are the most likely to take it, and the least likely to get well of it. The constant, or habitual use of liquor makes the system ripe, or ready for disease.

An English gentleman, who was in Russia, while the cholera was prevailing, says:—"It is a remarkable circumstance, that persons given to drinking were swept away like flies. In one town of twenty thousand inhabitants, every drunkard has fallen!—all are dead—not one remains!"

A physician in Poland, says:

the disease spared all those who led regular, temperate lives, and lived in healthy situations; but they who were weakened by drinking were always attacked. Out of every hundred individuals destroyed by cholera, it can be proved that NINETY were accustomed to the free use of ardent spirits."

A physician, who was in Montreal at the time the cholera was there, says, that "after there had been one thousand two hundred cases, it was found out that not a single drunkard who took it recovered; and that almost all who DID take it, had been at least moderate drinkers."

There were two hundred and four cases of cholera in the Park hospital, in New York, at one time. Of these, only SIX were temperate people. They all got well. Of the rest, one hundred and twenty-two died of the disease.

The cholera prevailed very badly in the city of Albany, in 1832. There were then five thousand members of the temperance society in that city. Only TWO of them died of the disease. There were twenty thousand persons there, not members of the temperance society. Among them there were three hundred and thirty-four deaths from cholera. Only think of this. Two deaths out of five thousand temperate people, and MORE THAN EIGHTY deaths out of every five thousand of those who were not temperate!

These facts prove very clearly

the point we are considering. They show that cold water helps to make a man strong and hearty, and keeps him free from sickness; while wines, and brandies, and all such drinks, weaken those who use them at all, and make them more likely to take disease.

And if those who never take enough to be made prisoners by this giant, who only venture on his grounds and walk about his castle, without ever getting fairly entrapped, are so much injured by the poison that comes forth from his dungeons; how must it be with those who are bound captives and kept in those dungeons?

Oh! then, we should fight against the giant Intemperance, and try to keep clear of him, BECAUSE HE IS AN ENEMY TO HEALTH AND STRENGTH.

The Third Reason for Fighting.

WE should fight against this Giant, BECAUSE HE IS AN ENEMY TO SAFETY AND HONOR.

The giant Intemperance exposes his prisoners to many dangers. He makes them unfit to take care of themselves. They do not know when they are in danger, and if they did, they are unable to avoid it. When one of them is walking, you expect every minute to see him tumble and break some of his bones. Look in the paper any morning, and you are almost sure to see an account of some poor man who has been run over by a locomotive, or drowned by falling off the wharf at night; — and nine times out of ten, if you ask how it happened, you will find that he was a captive of the giant. The only wonder is, that all his prisoners are not killed thus.

And, of course, if they are unable to care for themselves, they are unfit to take any care of others. Yet the lives of hundreds of men and women are often put in peril, and sometimes lost, by the influence of this giant on one or two persons.

Who would want to trust themselves at sea, with a captain and crew who were crazy? Who would want to travel in a train of cars, if they knew that the engineer and conductor were either crazy all the time, or subject at any time to spells of craziness? But a drunken man is no better than a crazy one. And a person in the habit of drinking, is liable at any moment to get drunk, and so to become crazy.

But the use of cold water keeps a man from thus losing his reason, and so enables him to see and avoid dangers. It promotes safety. How many of the steamboat explosions and shipwrecks occurring continually might be prevented, if the persons in charge of them were only cold water men!

Some time ago there was a steamboat plying on one of our western rivers. She was called the Fame. Captain Gordon, her commander, was a temperance man, and allowed no liquor to be kept, or used, by any of the officers or crew. About that time a new safety-valve for steam engines had been invented, which it was thought would tend to prevent explosions. It was called "Evan's Patent Safety-Valve." A good many people were unwilling to travel in any steamboat, unless it had one of these valves. One day a gentleman called on Captain Gordon in the cabin of his boat, and told him that he and twenty persons in his company were desirous of going on in his boat; "but," said the gentleman, " I can't do it, neither can my company; for I have been below examining your machinery, and I find you haven't got 'Evan's Patent Safety-Valve' attached to your engine. For this reason we can't go with you."

"I shall be very happy to have your company," said Captain Gordon. "Come below, and I will show you the best safety-valve in the world."

They walked down together to the engine-room. The captain stepped up to his sturdy engineer, and clapping him on the shoulder, said to the gentleman,—"There, sir, is my safety-valve—the best to be found anywhere;—a man who never drinks any thing but PURE COLD WATER!"

"You are right, captain," said the stranger; "I want no better safety-valve than that. We will come on board, sir."

Some years ago, a fine ship called the Neptune, with a crew of thirty-six men, sailed from the harbor of Aberdeen, in Scotland. It was early on a fine morning in May, when she started, with the fairest prospect of good weather and of a prosperous voyage. Not long after she had gone, the sky became cloudy. The wind changed. It came out directly ahead of the ship, and went on increasing in violence, till it blew a furious gale. By and by the Neptune was seen standing back towards the harbor, right before the wind, and with her sails set as though it was only blowing a fair, stiff breeze. She came bounding on before the storm, like a maddened war-horse. The tidings spread like lightning, and hundreds of people gathered on the pier to watch the strange sight. Something was wrong on board the ship. What COULD it be? The entrance to the harbor was very narrow, and beyond this were ledges of dangerous rocks. Over these the sea is now breaking in foam and thunder. Right on towards them the ship is hastening. What CAN be the matter? The people look on in silent horror. Now the ship rises on a mountain-wave,—and now she plunges into the foaming water. An attempt is made to shorten sail. It fails. She hastens on. A moment more, and hark! that thundering crash! The cry is heard — "She's lost! — She's lost!" She went to pieces. One man alone, of all on board, was saved. He lived to tell the dreadful secret. The giant was on board of that vessel. The crew were all intoxicated, and could not manage the vessel.

Thus we see that, while cold water promotes safety, there can be no safety where the giant Intemperance is allowed to come. He is an enemy to it.

And he is an enemy to HONOR, too. You can keep your honor if you keep to cold water. But get into the habit of drinking liquor, and your honor will soon be turned to shame. The giant Intemperance has such a bad name among men, that if you fall into his power your honor is lost. Every thing that is wicked, vile, and shameful, is associated with our thoughts of this giant. And he makes his prisoners so much like himself, that the same disgrace is fixed to their names. So that no matter how honored and respected a man has been before, as soon as he becomes a captive of this giant, he begins to lose his honor.

Men do not like to be called DRUNKARDS. The name is a mark of disgrace. It points them out as prisoners of this giant. But every one who drinks wine or liquor, is in danger of becoming a drunkard, and thus covering himself with shame and dishonor.

Every thing that is sinful, should be considered as a shame and disgrace. It's a shame for a man willingly to lose all his sense and reason, and act like a fool;—but this is what the drunkard does. It's a shame for a man to lose all proper feeling, and become as hard-hearted as a stone;—but this is what the drunkard does. It's a shame for a man to reel through the streets, and wallow in the gutter like a pig;—but this is what the drunkard does. It's a shame for a man to neglect his business, and spend his time in idleness; to leave his children beggars, and his wife a broken-hearted widow; —but this is what the drunkard does. It's a shame for a man to gamble, and rob, and murder, and commit all kinds of abominations;—but these are what the drunkard does.

Nearly all the people who live in our alms-houses, who are sent to our penitentiaries, and brought to the gallows, are led there by drinking. And those who use intoxicating liquors at all, are in danger of being led into any or all of these evils. Or if not led into them themselves, they are in danger of leading others into them. The giant Intemperance carries danger and disgrace with him. If you would live in safety and honor, put as wide a space between yourself and him as possible;—drink nothing that intoxicates, but keep to pure cold water.

This, then, is the third reason why we should resist this giant —— BECAUSE HE IS AN ENEMY TO SAFETY AND HONOR.

The Fourth Reason for Fighting.

WE should fight against this Giant, BECAUSE HE IS AN ENEMY TO COMFORT AND HAPPINESS.

Several years ago, when Barnum's Museum was on the corner of Seventh and Chestnut sts., Philadelphia, there was, in one of the rooms, a representation of a cold water drinker's home, and of a drunkard's home. These were placed side by side, so as to show the contrast more strongly. The figures were all of wax, and just about the size of living persons, so that it looked very real.

The first one represented a good sized room, with a neat carpet on the floor, and pretty paper on the walls. Two or three pictures were hanging against the sides of the room. A cheerful fire was burning in the grate. In the centre of the room stood a table with a snow-white cloth upon it. A tidy, happy-looking lady was spreading some very inviting things, for breakfast; while the largest of the children was bringing in a pitcher of water to fill the tumblers that were placed by every plate. An easy arm-chair was drawn up near the fire, and the father was leaning back in it, reading the morning paper, looking very snug and cosy in his wrapper and slippers. Around him a group of bright-eyed, rosy-cheeked little ones were playing, while a toddling boy was tugging at his father's gown, trying to climb up into his lap.

You did not need any one to tell you that comfort and happiness were there. Every thing looked so pleasant, that one almost felt like opening the door, and walking in to share their happiness. This was the cold water drinker's home.

Right next to it was the other scene. It was a room with bare floor, strewn with litter, and blackened with dirt. The plaster was falling from the walls and the ceiling. In the fireplace there were two or three half-burnt sticks, smouldering. An old bedstead stood in the corner, and a few ragged coverlets lay tumbled in a heap upon it. The rest of the furniture consisted of a table, and one or two rickety chairs. A loaf of bread partly cut, and a bottle on the table, were the only signs of a breakfast. The father, with his face unwashed, his beard unshaven, and his hair all tangled and matted, was beating a trembling child. The rest of the children were crowding up in the corner, pale and frightened, but each holding on to a dry crust of bread. Their faces were thin, and sickly. The mother sat upon the bed, her head between her hands, and her hair streaming wildly over her shoulders. Thin and tattered rags were the only clothes any of them had on. Misery and wretchedness were as plainly seen there, as if written with a sunbeam. This was the drunkard's home.

Children, which is the pleasantest picture? Which would you rather should be your home? All the difference was made by the PITCHER and the BOTTLE. The water in that pitcher had kept the giant Intemperance away from the first home; while the rum in the bottle had brought him into the other one. And it was because HE was there, that all was so wretched. He always drives comfort and happiness out from every house he enters. He turns gladness into sorrow, smiles into sighs, laughter into tears, wherever he goes. He makes his prisoners miserable themselves, and all about them unhappy too. Mothers and fathers, wives and children, brothers and sisters, suffer wherever he comes.

Let me tell you of a mother's sorrow, occasioned by a drunken son;—and of a whole family's sorrow, occasioned by a drunken husband and father.

A company of southern ladies, assembled in a parlor, were one day talking about their different troubles. Each one had something to say about her own trials. But there was one in the company, pale and sad looking, who for awhile said nothing. Suddenly rousing herself at last, she said:—

"My friends, you don't any of you know what trouble is."

"Will you please, Mrs. Gray," said the kind voice of one who knew her story, "tell the ladies what you call trouble?"

"I will, if you desire it; for, in the words of the prophet, 'I am the one who hath seen affliction.'

"My parents were very well off, and my girlhood was surrounded by all the comforts of life. Every wish of my heart was gratified, and I was cheerful and happy.

"At the age of nineteen I married one whom I loved more than all the world besides. Our home was retired; but the sun never shone upon a lovelier spot, or a happier household. Years rolled on peacefully. Five lovely children sat around our table, and a little curly head still nestled in my bosom. One night, about sundown, one of those fierce black storms came on which are so common to our southern climate. For many hours the rain poured down incessantly. Morning dawned, but still the elements raged. The country around us was overflowed. The little stream, near our dwelling, became a foaming torrent. Before we were aware of it, our house was surrounded by water. I managed, with my babe, to reach a little elevated spot, where the thick foliage of a few wide-spreading trees afforded some protection, while my husband and sons strove to save what they could of our property. At last a fearful surge swept away my husband, and he never rose again. Ladies, no one ever loved a husband more; but THAT was not trouble.

"Presently my sons saw their danger, and the struggle for life became the only consideration.

They were as brave, loving boys as ever blessed a mother's heart; and I watched their efforts to escape, with such agony as only mothers can feel. They were so far off that I could not speak to them; but I could see them closing nearer and nearer to each other, as their little island grew smaller and smaller.

"The swollen river raged fearfully around the huge trees. Dead branches, upturned trunks, wrecks of houses, drowning cattle, and masses of rubbish, all went floating past us. My boys waved their hands to me, and then pointed upwards. I knew it was their farewell signal; and you, mothers, can imagine my anguish. I saw them perish;— ALL perish. Yet that was not trouble.

"I hugged my baby close to my heart; and when the water rose to my feet, I climbed into the low branches of the tree, and so kept retiring before it, till the hand of God stayed the waters that they should rise no further.

I was saved. All my worldly possessions were swept away; all my earthly hopes blighted. Yet THAT was not trouble.

"My baby was all I had left on earth. I labored day and night to support him and myself, and sought to train him in the right way; but, as he grew older, evil companions won him away from me. He ceased to care for his mother's counsels; he would sneer at her kind entreaties and agonizing prayers. HE BECAME FOND OF DRINKING. He left my humble roof, that he might be unrestrained in his evil ways. And at last, one night, when heated by wine, he took the life of a fellow-creature. He ended his days upon the gallows! God had filled my cup of sorrow before; now, it ran over. THAT was trouble, my friends, such as I hope the Lord in mercy may spare you from ever knowing!"

Boys, girls, can you bear to think that you might bring such sorrow on your dear father, or mother? If you would not, be on your guard against the giant Intemperance. Let wine and liquors alone. Never touch them. That was a mother's sorrow.

Let us look at the sorrow brought on a family by the same dreadful evil.

Let me tell you an "old man's story."

Many years ago, a temperance meeting was held in a certain village. A little boy, who lived in the village, was very anxious to go, and persuaded his father to take him. The boy never forgot that meeting, and he wrote the account of it years afterwards. One of the speakers at the meeting was an old man. His hair was white, and his brow furrowed with age and sorrow. When he arose to speak, he said:—

"My friends, I am an old man, standing alone at the end of life's journey. Tears are in my eyes, and deep sorrow is in my heart. I am without friends, or home, or kindred on earth. It was not always so. Once

I had a mother. With her old heart crushed with sorrow, she went down to her grave. I once had a wife;—a fair, angel-hearted creature as ever smiled in an earthly home. Her blue eye grew dim, as the floods of sorrow washed away its brightness; and her tender heart I wrung till every fibre was broken. I once had a noble boy; but he was driven from the ruins of his home, and my old heart yearns to know if he yet lives. I once had a babe, a sweet, lovely babe;

but these hands destroyed it, and now it lives with Him who loveth the little ones. Do not spurn me, my friends," continued the old man. "There is light in my evening sky. The spirit of my mother rejoices over the return of her prodigal son. The injured wife smiles upon him who turns back again to virtue and honor. The child-angel visits me at nightfall, and I seem to feel his tiny hands upon my feverish cheek. My brave boy, if he yet lives, would forgive the sorrowing old man for treatment that drove him out into the world, and the blow that maimed him for life. God forgive me for the ruin I have brought upon all that were about me.

"I was a drunkard. From wealth and respectability, I plunged into poverty and shame. I dragged my family down with me. For years I saw the cheek of my wife grow pale, and her step grow weary. I left her alone to struggle for the children, while I was drinking and rioting at the tavern. She never complained, though she and the children often went hungry to bed.

"One New Year's night, I returned late to the hut where charity had given us shelter. My wife was still up, and shivering over the coals. I demanded food. She told me there was none, and then burst into tears. I fiercely ordered her to get some. She turned her eyes sadly upon me, the tears falling fast over her pale cheek. At this moment the child in its cradle awoke, and uttered a cry of hunger, startling the despairing mother, and making new sorrow in her breaking heart.

"'We have no food, James; —we have had none for several days. I have nothing for the babe. Oh! my once kind husband, must we starve?'

"That sad, pleading face, and those streaming eyes, and the feeble wail of the child, maddened me; and I—yes, I struck her a fierce blow in the face, and she fell forward upon the hearth. It seemed as if the furies of hell were raging in my bosom; and the feeling of the wrong I had committed added fuel to the flames. I had never struck my wife before, but now some terrible impulse drove me on, and I stooped down, as well as I could in my drunken state, and clenched both my hands in her hair.

"'For mercy's sake, James!' exclaimed my wife as she looked up into my fiendish countenance;—'You will not kill us; you will not harm Willie?' and she sprung to the cradle and grasped him in her arms. I caught her again by the hair and dragged her to the door, and as I lifted the latch, the wind burst in with a cloud of snow. With a fiendish yell, I still dragged her on, and hurled her out amid the darkness and storm. Then, with a wild laugh, I closed the door and fastened it. Her pleading moans and the sharp cry of her babe, mingled with the wail of the blast. But my horrible work was not yet complete.

"I turned to the bed where my oldest son was lying, snatched him from his slumbers, and, against his half-awakened struggles, opened the door and thrust him out. In the agony of fear he uttered that sacred name I was no longer worthy to bear. He called me — FATHER! and locked his fingers in my side-pocket. I could not wrench that grasp away; but, with the cruelty of a fiend, I shut the door upon his arm, and, seizing my knife, severed it at the wrist.

"It was morning when I awoke, and the storm had ceased. I looked round to the accustomed place for my wife. As I missed her, a dim, dark scene, as of some horrible nightmare, came over me. I thought it must be a fearful dream, but involuntarily opened the outside door with a shuddering dread. As the door opened, the snow burst in, and something fell across the threshold with a dull, heavy sound. My blood shot like melted lava through my veins, and I covered my eyes to shut out the sight. It was—O God! how horrible!—it was my own loving wife and her babe, frozen to death! With true mother's love, she had bowed herself over the child to shield it, and wrapped all her clothing around it, leaving her own person exposed to the storm. She had placed her hair over the face of the child, and the sleet had frozen it to the pale cheek. The frost was white on the lids of its half-opened eyes, and upon its tiny fingers.

"I never knew what became of my brave boy."

Here the old man bowed his head, and wept; and all in the house wept with him. Then, in the low tones of heart-broken sorrow, he concluded:—

"I was arrested, and for long months I was a raving maniac. When I recovered, I was sentenced to the penitentiary for ten years; but this was nothing to the tortures I have endured in my own bosom. And now I desire to spend the little remnant of my life in striving to warn others not to enter a path which has been so dark and fearful to me."

When the old man had finished, the temperance pledge was produced, and he asked the people to come forward and sign it. The father of the boy referred to leaped from his seat, and pressed forward to sign the pledge. As he took the pen in hand, he hesitated a moment.

"Sign it, young man, sign it," said the venerable speaker. "Angels would sign it. I would write my name in blood ten thousand times, if it would undo the ruin I have wrought, and bring back my loved and lost ones."

The young man wrote,— "Mortimer Hudson." The old man looked. He wiped his eyes, and looked again. His face flushed with fiery red, and then a death-like paleness came over it.

"It is — no, it cannot be; — yet how strange!" he muttered. "Pardon me, sir, but that was the name of my brave boy."

The young man trembled, and held up his left arm, from which the hand had been severed.

They looked for a moment in each other's eyes; and the old man exclaimed:—

"My own injured boy!"

The young man cried out:—

"My poor, dear father!"

Then they fell upon each other's neck and wept, till it seemed as if their souls would mingle into one.

Thus we see the misery and wretchedness this fearful giant Intemperance brings upon the drunkard, and upon all his family. If you love those at home, make up your minds that you will never cause them such sorrow and shame. Keep everything that intoxicates from your lips, and you will keep the giant from your home. Do so, BECAUSE HE IS AN ENEMY TO COMFORT AND HAPPINESS.

Those of you who have read ancient history, remember Hannibal, the great Carthaginian general. The Romans were the enemies of the Carthaginians. Hannibal's father had been general for many years, and had fought many battles against the Romans. He wanted his son to feel that they were his enemies, and that he must begin early to fight them. So, one day, when

Hannibal was about nine years old, his father gathered all the soldiers together. Then he went into his tent, and led out little Hannibal, and took him to the large altar where they used to offer sacrifices to their gods. Upon this altar he made him place his hand, and, in the presence of the whole army, swear that as long as he lived he would be an enemy to the Romans, and that he would fight against them with all his power.

Hannibal never forgot that

promise. He became the greatest enemy the Romans ever had.

Now, my dear children, you have a great many enemies. All these giants that we have been talking about are your enemies. They want to capture you, and they will try hard to do it. They are all strong, and fierce. But the last one, the giant Intemperance, is the greatest enemy to you of them all. And he is the strongest and most cruel of all. The sooner you feel this, the sooner you will be on your guard against him, and the more you will learn to hate him. And so I want you to do what Hannibal did. I want you to determine, NOW, while you are young, that, as long as you live, you will be an enemy of this giant, and fight against him with all your power. I want you to VOW LIFE-LONG WAR against him! Never make peace with him! Never give him any quarter.

I do not ask you to sign a pledge, but I do ask you all to resolve solemnly, that, by the help of God, you will never allow yourselves to drink wine, or liquor of any kind, unless you are sick, and it is given by the physician as a medicine. "TOUCH NOT—TASTE NOT—HANDLE NOT." This is the only safe course.

Those who do not follow this rule, often fall into the power of the giant Intemperance very suddenly, and when they least expect it; and, though they may escape again, do things, while they are his prisoners, that lead them into great trouble.

A man named John Cafree was shot in a fireman's quarrel in this city some time ago. The man who shot him was not an habitual drunkard. He was generally a sober, industrious man. But on that occasion he was tempted to drink too much, and now the dreadful guilt of murder is resting upon him.

Some years since there was a crowd gathered round a gallows, to see a young man hung. The sheriff took out his watch, and said:—"If you have anything to say, speak now, for you have only five minutes to live." The young man burst into tears, and said :—" Alas! and must I die? I had only one little brother. He had beautiful blue eyes, and flaxen hair, and I loved him. But one day I got drunk, for the first and only time in my life. On coming home I found my brother gathering strawberries in the garden. Without any sufficient cause I became angry with him, and struck him a blow with an iron rake. That blow killed him. I knew nothing about what was done till the next morning. On awaking from sleep I found myself tied, and guarded; and was told that when my little brother was discovered, he was dead, and his hair was clotted with blood and brains. Drinking liquor had done it. THAT has ruined me. I never was drunk but once, and now I am to hang for it. I have only one word more to say, and then I am going to stand before my Judge. I wish to say to young people — Never, never, never touch anything that can intoxicate." As he spoke these words he sprung from the scaffold, and was launched into eternity.

My dear boys, remember this warning. " Never touch anything that can intoxicate." And, my dear girls, do you remember it too. Don't think that because you are females you are in no danger. You ARE in danger.

In New York they are building a house for habitual drunkards, where they can be treated as sick or insane people are. Since this building has been started, nearly three thousand confirmed drunkards have applied for admission. Among these are between FOUR AND FIVE HUNDRED FEMALES FROM THE MOST RESPECTABLE FAMILIES. ALL persons, who drink wine or liquor AT ALL, are in danger both of becoming drunkards themselves, and of making others drunkards by their example. Drink cold water, and you are in no danger. The giant Intemperance will never be able to make you his prisoner, if you keep to cold water.

Now, how many giants have we spoken of? Five. What was the first? The GIANT HEATHENISM. How are we to fight him? BY THROWING THE STONES OF TRUTH AT HIM. What was the second? THE GIANT SELFISHNESS. How are we to fiight him? BY SELF-DENIAL. What was the third? THE GIANT COVETOUSNESS. How are we to fight him? BY LEARNING TO GIVE. What was the fourth? THE GIANT ILL-TEMPER. How are we to fight him? BY LEARNING TO BE LIKE JESUS. What was the fifth? THE GIANT INTEMPERANCE. And how are we to fight him? BY DRINKING COLD WATER. We had four good reasons why we should fight this giant. What are they? We ought to fight him; BECAUSE COLD WATER IS THE DRINK THAT GOD HAS MADE FOR US:— BECAUSE HE IS AN ENEMY TO HEALTH AND STRENGTH; TO SAFETY AND HONOR; TO COMFORT AND HAPPINESS.

In conclusion, my dear children, I want you all to become brave giant fighters. Fighting, in general, is poor business. For men and women, or boys and girls, to be fighting among themselves is a shameful thing. But to be fighting these giants is very different. This is proper for girls as well as boys; for ladies as well as gentlemen. It is a right thing, a brave thing, an honorable thing. But do not try to fight them in your own strength, or else you are sure to be beaten

David prayed to God to help him when he became a giant fighter. It was this which made him successful. And you must do the same. Pray for Jesus to help you. Then go at the giants with all your might, and He will "teach your hands to war and your fingers to fight;" and will bring you off, at last, "conquerors, and more than conquerors."

WONDERFUL THINGS.

I.

THE WONDERFUL STAFF.

"Thy rod and thy staff they comfort me." — PSALM xxiii. 4.

IF you are travelling along a rough road, or climbing up a mountain, it is a great help and comfort to have a good strong staff to lean on. When persons are travelling in Switzerland, they have a particular kind of staff, called an alpenstock. It is often ornamented at the upper end with the horn of a chamois, or

Swiss-goat; while the lower end has an iron point fastened to it, so that in climbing up, or passing over slippery places, travellers, by striking it in the ice, can keep themselves from falling, as they lean on it, or steady themselves by it.

In the verse in which our text is found, David is speaking of dying. He compares it to walking through a dark valley, which he calls "the valley of the shadow of death." If we had to walk through such a valley, where there were many deep pits and slippery places, it would be a great comfort to have a good stout staff, by the help of which we could make our way along in safety amidst all the surrounding dangers. David tells us here that God has provided such a staff for His people. He says, "Thy rod and thy staff, they comfort me."

The staff here spoken of means the Bible, or the Word of God. This is like a staff which God wishes His people to lean on. And if we learn to use it rightly, we shall find it a great help to us. Here, then, we have another of the Bible Wonders. Our subject now is,— *The Wonderful Staff*. The Bible is a wonderful staff because of its power to do *three* things for us.

In the first place, it is wonderful for its POWER TO PROTECT.

David, who wrote the text, was a shepherd before he was a king. And in trying to protect his sheep, he must sometimes have had very hard work to do, and very great dangers to meet. There were wild beasts in Palestine when David was living. One day, while he was watching his sheep, a lion sprang into his flock, picked up a lamb, and walked away with it. David was a brave boy. He had a tender, loving heart, too. He could not bear to think of his dear little lamb being torn in pieces, and eaten by the lion.

So he jumped up and ran after him. That was before fire-arms were invented. David had no gun. He has not told us what arms he had. I suppose he certainly had a good stout shepherd's staff. It is very likely that he had also a sort of sheath knife, such as our sailors have, fastened to a girdle round his waist. With no other weapons than these, I suppose, he started after the lion. Would you not like to have seen him fighting the lion? I should, very much. We can fancy we see it. There is the lion getting away as quick as he can. But he cannot get on very fast, for the lamb is heavy. And here comes David after him, hallooing and shouting, and hoping to make him drop the lamb, and run off. But the lion is hungry, so he holds on to the lamb. And now David is close up to him. He lifts up his heavy staff and hits him a tremendous blow on his hollow side. The lamb is dropped. The lion turns on David with a terrific roar. He is too close to spring on him, but he rises on his hind feet, and opens his huge jaws to devour him. Quick as thought David drops his staff. He seizes the lion by the beard with his left hand, and taking his knife in the right hand, he plunges it into the monster's side, again and again, till, with a faint growl, the lion falls dead to the ground.

But we have a higher authority than David to show us how to use God's Word so as to protect us from our enemies. Our blessed Saviour has left us an example here. He had a fight, when He was on earth, worse than that of David with the lion. You know we read that "Jesus was led up of the Spirit into the wilderness to be tempted of the devil." (Matt. iv. 1.) That temptation was like a fight with Satan. It was a long fight. It lasted forty days and forty nights. And the only weapon that Jesus made use of was this very staff of which we are speaking. Every time that Satan tempted Him to do what was wrong, Jesus answered him with a text of Scripture. And when He did this it was like hitting him a blow with this wonderful staff. He made use of the Word of God just as a man, when attacked, uses a staff to ward off the strokes of his enemy, and to hit him, in return, stout, staggering blows, that may drive him from the field. Jesus found God's Word a wonderful staff for His own protection.

And so His people often find it. I met with an interesting story lately, which illustrates this part of our subject very strikingly.

Some years ago there was a forester, named Grimez, who lived in a lonely place in the thick woods of the Silesian mountains, in Prussia. His family consisted of his wife and his mother, with a little daughter, about seven years of age. His wife and mother were good Christian women; but he himself was not a Christian. He did not even believe the Bible, and often used to ridicule his wife for her prayers, and what he called " her foolish trust in God."

The time to which our story refers was a dark and stormy evening in autumn. The wind whistled mournfully through the trees of the forest. The two women and the little child sat round the fire in their house. The forester had not yet come home from the neighboring town, to which he had gone in the morning. The family were beginning to feel very anxious about him. And they had good cause to feel so. It seemed that a band of robbers had been infesting that part of the forest of late, and had made it very unsafe. This forester was the officer of the King of Prussia. His duty was to take care of the forest. After long efforts he had just succeeded in capturing all this band of robbers, except their leader. He was a very strong, and cunning, but wicked man. And he had vowed to have his revenge on the forester and his family, for breaking up his band. The women of that lonely family knew this. No wonder that they felt very anxious as they sat round the fire on that stormy evening. They could think and talk of nothing else but the dangers that surrounded them, and the absent head of their family.

At last the grandmother said it

would do no good to go on talking so, and giving way to their fears; and that it would be much better to seek comfort from God's Word, and ask the protection of Him, without whose will not even a sparrow can fall to the ground.

Then the wife brought out their family Bible and read aloud from it the seventy-first psalm. These are some of the words that she read. They were wonderfully appropriate to their circumstances:—"In thee, O Lord, do I put my trust; let me never be put to confusion. Be thou my strong habitation whereunto I may continually resort; for thou art my rock and my fortress. *Deliver me, O my God, out of the hand of the wicked, out of the hand of the unrighteous and cruel man."*

When the psalm was finished she read an evening hymn in keeping with the psalm. After singing this they knelt down together in prayer. They told God about their fears, and asked Him to protect them, as well as their beloved husband and father. They prayed for the poor and the sick of their parish; for all evil-doers, and especially for the wicked robber in their neighborhood, that the Lord would have mercy on him, and change his heart, and turn him from his evil ways.

After this their fears were gone, and they felt calm and comfortable. They had hardly finished their prayers, when they heard the well-known footsteps of him they were looking for approaching the house. He was brought home in safety. They were all very glad of this; for while they had been so uneasy about him, he had been feeling very much the same about them, fearing lest the robber might come and kill them while he was away. So he, too, felt very happy to find his family safe and well.

Before they went upstairs to bed the forester's wife told him how anxious they had felt about him during the evening, and how they had prayed to God to take care of him and of themselves. He smiled, as he had often done before, and said she was a foolish woman to think there was any use in praying. For his part he preferred to trust to his good weapons, and to his faithful dogs. Then he examined the doors and windows to see that they were fastened; he loaded his fire-arms and unchained his dogs, and thought that he could lie down and sleep without any cause for fear.

Well, an hour or two has passed away. All is quiet in the forester's house. The family are fast asleep. No sound is heard but the rustling of the trees as the wind sweeps through them. But hark! what is that? There is a movement — a quick movement — in the room where the forester's family had been spending the evening. And now, look; there is a man — a desperate looking man — creeping out from under the settle, or old wooden bench, which stood there. It is the robber they were so much afraid of. He had managed to steal in about sundown, when nobody saw him, and to hide himself under the settle. There he had heard all that had been said. He had come in to have his revenge by murdering the whole family in their sleep. He looks round carefully on all sides, and listens. Not a sound is heard. Now there is nothing to prevent him from carrying out his purpose. Ah! yes, but there is, though. He goes softly and silently to the table. He lays down on it a large, sharp knife, which he has brought with him. The rays of the full moon are shining through an opening in the window-shutter into the room. He picks up the Bible, which the forester's wife had read from at their evening worship, and which lay there open still at the seventy-first psalm. The words of that psalm have had a wonderful effect upon him. He tries to read them over again in the feeble light of the moon; but it is too dark to see them, so he shuts up the book. Then he stands by the table for a few moments, hesitating what he had better do. Two or three times he picks up the knife, and resolves to have his revenge by plunging it into the bosom of the sleepers upstairs. But each time he lays the knife down again. Something seems to hold him back. He thinks of the words of that wonderful psalm, and he is afraid to do it. Then he goes to the window and opens it very gently. He unfastens the shutter without making the slightest noise. He leaves the knife on the table, but takes the Bible in his hand; he gets up on the window-ledge, and creeps out so cautiously that even the watch-dogs, which seem to have fallen asleep, neither see nor hear him. Then he jumps over the garden hedge, and in a few moments he disappears in the dark shadows of the wood.

When the forester and his family came down the next morning and found the window open, and a great sharp knife lying on the table, and the Bible gone, they were, of course, very much surprised. They could not possibly explain it. The open window showed that somebody had been in the house. The great knife showed that his object had been murder; while the missing Bible seemed to show that somehow or other *that* had been the means of saving them. The whole house was searched, yet nothing else was missing but the Bible. What did it mean? It was a mystery which no one could explain. The pious wife thanked God for their protection. Even her unbelieving husband could not help seeing that it was neither his dogs nor his guns that had saved them. He stopped laughing at his wife, and began to think that there was something in religion after all. Nothing more was ever seen of the robber in that neighborhood. But this is only half the story. The other half of it will illustrate another part of our sermon. I will give it you then. What I have now told illustrates this first part very well.

It shows us how God made use of His Word for the protection of that family. This was the staff with which He drove the murderer away. This is indeed a wonderful staff. It is wonderful for its power to *protect*.

In the second place, it is wonderful for its power TO COMFORT.

If you have a long journey to take, and feel faint and weary, it is a great help and comfort to have a good strong staff that you can lean upon. Well, God's Word is like a staff for this reason. It gives strength to His people when they feel weak and ready to faint under their labors or their trials.

In the early days of Christianity, you know, the followers of Jesus had to bear a great deal of persecution. On one occasion a Christian young man was ordered to be tortured, to make him give up his religion. First, he was hung over a slow fire to scorch his feet; then he was bound to a post, and his flesh was torn with red-hot pincers. But he bore these, and other horrible cruelties, without a cry or a groan. Finding that he would not give up his religion, his enemies let him go.

When his friends came round him they asked him how he could bear those dreadful sufferings so patiently.

"It was painful, indeed," said the noble youth, "but it seemed to me as if there were an angel standing at my side all the time, who kept pointing to heaven, and whispering promises like these in my ear:

"Fear not, I am with thee; I will strengthen thee, yea, I will help thee." "When thou passest through the waters, I will be with thee; when thou walkest through the fire thou shalt not be burned; neither shall the flame kindle upon thee."

That young man was leaning on this wonderful staff, and he found that it had power to comfort him.

One day a Bible-reader was climbing up a broken staircase, which led to a garret, in one of the worst parts of London. When he got up to the last landing-place he saw a very savage looking man, who stood, with folded arms, leaning against the wall.

"My friend," said the visitor, holding a Bible in his hand, "here is a book that tells us the secret of true happiness; won't you let me read out of it a little for you?"

The man looked at him very fiercely, and said, "Get out with your nonsense, or I'll kick you down-stairs."

He tried to soften him, but in vain.

While this was going on he heard a feeble voice, which seemed to come from one of the broken doors that opened on the landing, saying, "Come in here with your book."

He pushed the door open and entered the room. It was a wretched looking place. There was no furniture in it but a three-legged stool, and a bundle of straw in a corner. On this straw an aged woman was lying, with her thin and wasted limbs.

When the visitor entered she raised herself on one elbow, and, fixing her eyes eagerly on him, she said,—

"Does your book tell about the blood that cleanseth from all sin?" He sat down on the stool by her side and said,—

"My poor friend, why do you

want to know about the blood that cleanseth from all sin?" With a voice of fearful earnestness, she replied,—

"Why do I want to know about it? Man, I am dying; I am going to stand before God. I have been a wicked woman, a very wicked woman, all my life. I shall have to answer for every thing I have done:" and she groaned bitterly at the thought of her sins. "But once," she went on to say, "once, some years ago, in passing by the door of a church I went in for a moment, I don't know why. I came out directly, and went away;

but one word I heard then I have never forgotten. It was something about the blood that cleanseth from all sin. Tell me, oh, tell me, is there any thing in your book about that blood?"

The visitor answered her by opening his Bible, and reading the first chapter of the First Epistle of St. John, in which occur the precious words, "The blood of Jesus Christ, His Son, cleanseth us from all sin." The poor creature seemed to devour the words as they fell from his lips, and when he stopped at the end of the chapter, she said: "Read more, read more." He read through the second chapter. Then he heard a slight noise. On looking round, who should he see there but the savage looking man who had threatened to knock him down-stairs, and who was the poor woman's son. He was listening eagerly, and the tears were trickling down his face. The visitor read on through the third, fourth, and fifth chapters before the poor listener would allow him to stop. Then she would not let him go till he promised to come again the next day. He went the next day, and every day after for three weeks. Every day the son followed the visitor into his mother's room, and listened attentively to all that was said. Then the poor woman died in peace. As soon as she understood what was meant by the cleansing blood she believed it. She felt sure that it took all her sins away, and this made her very happy. She went down to her grave leaning on this wonderful staff, and, oh! how it comforted her!

On the day of her funeral, as the visitor stood by, while they were filling up the grave, the son of the poor woman beckoned him aside. He, too, had found pardon and peace through the same precious blood. When he had taken the visitor aside he said to him: "Sir, I have been thinking that there is nothing I should like so much as to spend the rest of my life in telling others of the blood that cleanseth from all sin."

How natural this was! He had found comfort himself from leaning on this wonderful staff, and he wished to get others to use it too, and enjoy the comfort of it.

He became a Bible-reader and visitor among the poor.

This is a wonderful staff. The second reason why it is so is, because of its power to comfort.

It is a wonderful staff, in the

third place, because of its POWER TO SAVE.

We read in one place in the Bible that " the Word of God is *able to save the soul.*" — James i. 21. And when one who felt that he was a sinner came to St. Paul, with the question, " What must I do to be saved?" his answer was, " Believe on the Lord Jesus Christ, and thou shalt be saved." This means — believe what the Bible tells you about Jesus. Believe that He died for our sins, and that because He did this God is ready to pardon and save all who are willing to be saved in this way. When Paul said to the Philippian jailer, " Believe on the Lord Jesus Christ, and thou shalt be saved," it was just the same as if he had offered him this wonderful staff, of which we are speaking, and had said to him, " Here, take this staff. Keep firm hold of it. Lean all your weight upon it, and it will save your soul." This is the one thing, above all others, that makes this a wonderful staff.

And now we have just reached the place where the other half of our story about the robber and the forester comes in nicely.

The robber was never seen or heard of in the forest after that night. Sometime after that, in the year 1813, there was war among the different nations of Europe. The French and Prussians were fighting against each other. The king of Prussia had raised a large army. Grimez, our forester, had a position as captain in this army. The French army had taken a strong position in a part of the country where there were several lakes, all the shores of which were covered with dense woods. On the borders of the largest of these lakes were several huts inhabited by fishermen. The Prussian army was ordered to drive the French away from that position. This led to a very severe battle. The Prussians gained the victory, and drove the French away. But they gained it with the loss of a great many men. Among those who fell, on that day, was our brave captain, the forester. His men thought he was killed, and left him on the field for dead. But he was only badly wounded. After his friends had gone he lay groaning in pain among the dead. A fisherman was coming cautiously up in his boat, to see if a little hut of his on the shore had been destroyed by the army. He heard the groans of the wounded man. He rowed his boat to land,

and went up to the spot from which the cry of pain was heard.

He found the Prussian officer lying in his blood. He gave a low whistle, and some of his companions came up from the boat. They carried the wounded man to their boat, and rowed him to the opposite shore of the lake, about two miles distant. They landed in the neighborhood of several cottages. Into one of these the wounded man was carried. The fisherman and his wife received him with great kindness. They dressed his wounds and nursed him with tender care. At first it seemed doubtful whether he would recover; but finally the fever left him, and he began to get better. The fisherman wrote to the captain's family to tell them how he was. His wife and daughter came to nurse him, and be with him. The fisherman and his wife gave them the use of their cottage, and they stayed with one of their neighbors till the soldier got well.

As he lay upon his sick bed he could not help thinking of all that had happened to him. He thought of the wonderful way in which God had protected himself and his family from the robber on that memorable night. He thought of the way in which he had been taken care of, when left for dead on the battle field. He saw God's hand in it all. He was led to pray to Him earnestly, and became a Christian.

And now he was well enough to go home. He thanked the kind fisherman for all that he had done for him, and wished to pay him for the great trouble he had caused him. But to their surprise he would take nothing. When they pressed it on him, he said he was much more indebted to them than they were to him. He said further that he had a great treasure of theirs which he had once taken away, and now wished to restore. Then he went to a closet and brought out a Bible. As soon as the forester's wife saw it she recognized it as their dear old Bible which had disappeared so strangely on that night that never could be forgotten. She caught it eagerly in her hands, and pressed it to her bosom. Then the fisherman told them the following story: — "I see you don't recognize me," looking at the forester, "but I am the robber that caused such trouble in your neighborhood, till you caught my companions, and had them put in prison. I was very angry with you for this, and swore to have revenge on you. I crept into your house about dark one evening, intending to murder you and all your family at night while asleep. All that evening I lay under the settle in your sitting-room, waiting for the hour when I could carry out my cruel purpose. Against my will I was obliged to hear the seventy-first psalm which your wife read aloud. It had a wonderful effect on me. When I heard her prayers I felt worse still. It seemed as if an unseen hand was laid upon me, to keep me back from doing what I had come to do. I felt that I could not do that now. All my desire then was to get that wonderful book and read it. I left your house without doing what I had gone there to do. But I took your Bible with me. I thought there must be more words of wonder in the book than I had heard that evening. For weeks I kept hid in the woods near your home. The Bible was my companion in my solitude. As I read it I saw what a great sinner I was, and what a great Saviour there is in Jesus. I sought Him, and found Him. That same Saviour who pardoned the thief on the cross had mercy on me, and received me into His kingdom. Then I left that part of the country, and found employment with a fisherman in this neighborhood. As God had made me a new man I wished to begin a new life. I am living very happily here. My excellent wife is helping me to serve God. We have all that we want for this world, and a blessed hope for the next. And all this I owe to the Bible I found in your house that evening. You, forester, trusted to your guns and your dogs. They could not have helped you any. Your life and the lives of your family were in my hand. Nothing but God's Word saved you. It was only that which kept my hand from seizing the knife and plunging it into your bosoms. It was that which protected you and your family then; and it is that which has saved you from the battle field now. Don't thank me; but thank that merciful God who made use of His blessed Word to save both you and me."

Such was the fisherman's story. The tears that were flowing down the faces of the forester and his wife showed how much they were affected by all God's wonderful goodness to them. With full hearts they thanked the fisherman for all his care and kindness to them. Then they returned to their home a very happy family. As they sat round their table, on the first night of their return, that precious Bible was brought out again. The seventy-first psalm was read over once more; and as he read it aloud to his family the forester thought that these words in the psalm seemed very surprising:—" I am as a wonder unto many, but Thou art my strong refuge. Let my mouth be filled with Thy praise, and with Thy honor all the day long."

Thus we see how God's Word is indeed a wonderful staff. It is wonderful because of its power to do three things. These are, to *protect* — to *comfort* — to *save*.

Be sure you take this staff with you, and learn how to use it. Then you will be happy here, and happy in heaven for ever.

II.

THE WONDERFUL COMFORTER.

"As one whom his mother comforteth, so will I comfort you." — ISAIAH lxvi. 13.

THE word *mother* is one of the sweetest words in our language. It has more power over us than any other. It would be easy to give many facts to prove this. Let me mention one. During the late war, a chaplain was going through the wards of a hospital, to talk and pray with the sick and wounded soldiers. Among them was a Scotchman who had been a very wicked man; he would never allow any one to talk to him on the subject of religion. On coming to his bedside the chaplain said to him,— "Well, Donald, how are you to-day?"

"Better, sir, I thank you."

"Shall I read a few verses to you from the New Testament?"

Donald turned his face to the wall and said nothing. The chaplain sat down by his cot and began to sing the old Scotch version of the twenty-third psalm,—

> "The Lord's my shepherd, I'll not want,
>   He maketh me down to lie
> In pastures green. He leadeth me
>   The quiet waters by."

Now Donald had been blessed with a pious mother. When he was a child she had taught him to read the Bible, and instructed him in its blessed truths. She had been a good, kind, loving mother to her boy. And though he had not followed her teachings, but had forgotten God, and had run to great lengths in his wicked ways, yet in the midst of all his sinful doings he never could forget his mother. And the thought of her melted his heart in a way that nothing else could do. She had been dead, and in heaven, for many years. She had had a very gentle voice, and sang sweetly the old Scotch psalms; and this twenty-third psalm, which the chaplain was singing by the soldier's bedside, was his mother's favorite psalm. Donald had often, when a little boy, sat on his mother's knee, and leaned his head on her loving breast, while she sang that sweet and precious psalm. He had not heard it for many long years. As soon as the chaplain began to sing it his heart grew tender. He thought of the home of his childhood. He thought of his sainted mother, now in heaven. He thought of her love for him; of the tears he had seen her shed, and the prayers he had heard her offer for him. He thought of all his sins; and as the chaplain went on singing, the big tears were fast rolling down his cheeks. When the psalm was finished, he turned to the chaplain and asked for a prayer. So he "told him the old, old story of Jesus and His love;" and then he kneeled down and prayed with him. That was the turning-point in Donald's life. From that time he became a changed man. He turned from his wicked ways, and tried to live so that he might meet his mother in heaven.

Here we see how God made use of the wonderful power of a mother's love and a mother's influence to bring back this wandering son into the right path.

When we are children, our mother is the one to whom we are accustomed to run first for comfort if any thing troubles us. She is always ready to take us into her arms; to listen to the story of our griefs; to wipe our tears gently away, and try to make us feel comfortable and happy.

And this is the reason why God compares Himself to a mother, and says, "As one whom his mother comforteth, so will I comfort you." While we are in this world we shall always have trouble of one kind or another; and so we shall always need some one to comfort us. But our mothers cannot always be with us. And even if they could, there are many sorrows and troubles in which they have no power at all to comfort us. And this is the reason why God Himself offers to be our Comforter. And in doing this He promises to be as tender, kind, and loving as a mother. This is what He means when He says, "As one whom his mother comforteth, so will I comfort you."

Here we have another of the *Bible Wonders*. We are to speak now about the *Wonderful Comforter.* God is a wonderful Comforter because He is always present; because He has so many to serve Him, and because there is so much He can do, that no matter what our trouble is, He can always help and comfort us under it. He can make use of all the angels in heaven, and all the people in the world, and all the things written in the Bible to comfort His people when they are in trouble. Oh, God is indeed a wonderful Comforter! There are many occasions when we need comfort; but I will only speak now of *three* of these, in which God proves a wonderful Comforter to His people.

The first of these is, TIMES OF DANGER.

There are so many dangers about us in this world, that we always need such a Comforter. We cannot always see these dangers, and therefore we do not always feel the need of a comforter. But as soon as the danger appears we must have a com forter, or we are wretched. This is the reason why Jesus said to His disciples, "I will not leave you comfortless: I will come to you." The way in which Jesus comes to His people now, to comfort them, is by sending His blessed Spirit into their hearts. This Spirit helps us to understand what the Bible teaches about Jesus, and this gives us comfort. And when the Holy Spirit whispers into our hearts some of the sweet promises of the Bible in a gentle, loving way, then Jesus is proving Himself a wonderful Comforter; and then He is fulfilling the promise of the text, when He says, "As one whom his mother comforteth, so will I comfort you."

Here is a story about a little girl, and how she found comfort when in danger.

One morning a Christian lady, who was engaged in teaching, went to her pleasant school-room and found many of her scholars absent. Two of the little ones, who had been in school a few days before, were then lying still and cold in death, and others were very sick. That fearful disease diphtheria had entered the village and the school.

The children were weeping bitterly as the teacher entered, and some of them came up to her at once, and said, "O, teacher, Minnie and Georgie are dead! What shall we do? Do you think we shall be sick and die?"

She gently rang the bell, as a signal for opening school, and when they had all taken their seats, she said, —

"Children, you are all alarmed on account of this terrible disease. You are grieving for the death of your schoolmates, and are fearing lest you too may be taken. Some of you have asked me, '*What* shall we do?' I know of only one way to escape this trouble, and that is to *hide* from it. If you will listen I will read to you about a hiding-place."

They all listened attentively while she read the ninety-first psalm. It begins in this way : — "He that dwelleth in the secret place of the Most High shall abide under the shadow of the Almighty. I will say of the Lord, He is my refuge and my fortress; my God, in Him will I trust. He shall cover thee with His feathers, and under His wings shalt thou trust; His truth shall be thy shield and buckler," etc. The teacher did not say a word about the psalm, but she offered a short prayer in which she asked God to comfort them all in that time of danger. The scholars all seemed hushed by the sweet words of the psalmist, and the lessons went on as usual.

At noon a sweet little girl named Lizzie came to her, and said, — "Teacher, are *you* afraid of the diphtheria?"

"No," said the teacher.

"Well, but shouldn't you, if you thought you should get sick, and die?"

"No, dear, I trust not," was the reply.

Lizzie stopped questioning, and looked her teacher full in the face for a few minutes with thoughtful, wondering eyes; then her face brightened a little, and she said,—

"Oh, I know now, I know why you are not afraid. You are hiding under God's wings, that you read about in the psalm this morning. What a nice hiding-place that must be! I thought as you read the chapter, how I should like to hide there too! Then I should not be afraid of diphtheria, or any thing else." And Lizzie's eyes filled up with tears, as she asked,—

"O, teacher, is there room for *me* there?"

"Yes, Lizzie," was the answer, "there's room for you, and for every one who wishes to come. Jesus, whose wings make this hiding-place, longs to *hide* you in His arms, to clasp you to His heart, and to wash you from your sins in His own blood. And though He is used to hear the songs of thousands of angels up in heaven, yet it will be sweeter than the music of their songs to hear your child-like voice whispering to Him, 'Jesus, Thou art my hiding-place!' Will you not say these words with your whole heart?"

"*I will*," was Lizzie's soft, but decided answer. She made Jesus her hiding-place that day. And "as one whom his mother comforteth, so did God comfort her."

God is a wonderful Comforter in times of danger.

But He is so, secondly, IN TIMES OF WANT.

These times come very often.

We are always in want of something or other. Every moment that we live our breasts are rising and falling. What are we doing, all the time, that keeps up this motion? Breathing. And what do we breathe? Air. Could we live without air? No. Could I speak to you without air? No. Could you hear me without air? No. So you see we want air all the time. But could we live on air alone? When hungry, if you were told to go and take a good dinner of air, would *that* satisfy you? No. When we are hungry what do we want? Food. And when we are thirsty what do we want? Water. And when cold weather comes, and we are almost naked, what do we want? Clothing.

But these things we can generally get without much trouble. God has made the air so plenty that we can get as much as we want without paying any thing for it. It is in the streets. It comes into our houses and churches. It is about us wherever we are, by night and by day, so that even when we are asleep we can get as much air as we need. Food and clothing are not quite so plentiful as air. We have to work for them. Yet when we are well, if we are industrious and careful, we can generally secure them.

But sometimes sickness comes, and we are not able to work. Or even if not sick, we may not be able to get work to do. Then we can buy neither food nor clothing. And when our children have to go hungry to bed, because there is nothing in the house for them to eat; when they wake in the morning, crying for bread, and there is none to give, then *that* is a time of want indeed. And at such times Jesus is a wonderful Comforter to His people.

Now let me give you a story to show what a wonderful Comforter

Jesus is to His people in times of want. It is a story about "The Last Dollar."

Some years ago there was a minister who had charge of a little church in a mountain village of New England. He was poor, and ministered to a congregation in which were no rich people. He had a wife and three children. Though often in great poverty he had never been reduced to his last dollar. But now this was his sad case. He handed it to his wife, with a sigh, and said, —

"It is our *last* dollar, my dear. But the Lord will provide."

"You've always been saying that, husband," said his wife, as the tears filled her eyes; "but what is to become of us when this is gone? They won't trust us any more at the store; and your salary won't be due for three weeks, even if you get it then. Why do you stay here, James, when we can't get bread for our children?"

"I have no other place to go to," said her husband, "nor money to travel with, if the way was open. My work for the present is here. The Bible tells us that God 'feedeth the young ravens.' Let us trust Him, dear Mary. Surely He will take care of us."

"I wish I had faith like yours, James," said his wife; "but I haven't, and it won't come to me. Oh! what shall I do for my poor children?" she cried, in tones of deep distress.

"David said, 'I have been young, and now am old,'" replied her husband, "'yet saw I never the righteous forsaken, nor his seed begging their bread.' That promise has never failed yet, and I don't believe it will fail now. Let us trust God, my dear wife, and not be afraid."

Just as he ceased speaking there was a sudden knock at the door. While this conversation was going on between the minister and his wife, a violent storm had been raging outside. On opening the door, a traveller, wet through with the rain, entered the room.

"I was coming through the forest," said he, "when overtaken by the storm, and ventured to stop at the first house I saw for shelter. My horse is in the stable. I hope I have not taken too great a liberty?"

"O, by no means, my dear sir," said the minister. "We have but a poor shelter, as you see; but such as it is you are welcome to it; here is a good fire at any rate to dry your wet things."

It was in the kitchen where this conversation took place. They could only afford to keep one fire; so *that* room had to serve them as kitchen, dining-room, and study. .

The stranger proved to be an educated, wealthy gentleman. The minister had a long talk with him about many things of which he did not feel at liberty to speak to any of the people of his church.

At last the storm was over. The stranger having thoroughly dried his clothing, rose to go. He thanked the good man and his wife for the shelter kindly afforded him. The minister brought out his horse, went with him to the gate, and, after bidding him good-by, stood and watched him till he disappeared behind a turn of the road.

Then he went back into the house. As soon as he entered the room, his wife said, "See here, James, I found this on the table near where the gentleman sat."

It was a fifty dollar note, wrapped hastily up in a bit of paper that looked as if it had been torn from a pocket-book, and on the inside of the paper was written the verse from the psalms which the minister had repeated to his wife just before the knock was heard. "I have been young, and now am old, yet saw I never the righteous forsaken, nor his seed begging their bread." The stranger had overheard what had been said, and he had left this money to show that God was still faithful to His promises.

"I thought he was writing the direction he asked me for," said the minister. "He means this for us. Thanks be to the Lord! Did I not tell you, my dear, He would provide?"

His wife burst into tears.

"God forgive me!" she said. "I never will doubt Him again. The Lord surely sent this stranger to help us."

"And He will still provide," said her husband. "Whatever my lot may be, here or elsewhere, in Him will I trust."

About a month after this, a letter came one day to the post-office of that village, addressed to this minister, whose name was the Rev. James Spring. When he opened it, he read as follows:—

"REV. AND DEAR SIR:— The church at Maryville has unanimously ehosen you to be its pastor. The salary is fifteen hundred dollars, and a good parsonage."

The letter then went on to say that

"the writer first came to know you by seeking shelter in your house during a storm, a few weeks since. He overheard you, in a time of great distress and want, speak with such firm faith in the promises of God's Word, that he feels sure you are just the person to take charge of this church, and it is on his recommendation that you have been called."

Maryville was the county town, a rich and thriving place, in the midst of a broad and fertile valley at the foot of the hills, up among which this good minister had been laboring for several years in poverty and want. He was very successful and happy in his new parish, and always had money enough to provide what was necessary for the comfort of his family. He never forgot the lesson God taught him on that stormy day. And often when he met with people who showed a want of faith he would tell them the story of his Last Dollar.

This story beautifully illustrates the point before us. It was a time of want to that minister and his family, when their money was spent and there was no prospect of more for weeks to come. But, "as one whom his mother comforteth, *so* did

God comfort them." And see how much pains He took to do it! If God had sent an angel from heaven to take a fifty dollar note and place it on that minister's table, or put it into his hands and say, "The Lord of heaven sends you this," *that* would have seemed very wonderful. And yet I think the way in which He did send it was still more wonderful. It would have been easier for God, as it seems to us, to have sent an angel to carry this money to the minister than to have sent it in the way He did. As it was, God had to send this gentleman on a journey through that part of the country on that very day. He did not know the minister, and had no intention of stopping at his house. So God sent that storm to burst and beat upon the traveller, in order to bring him, drenched and dripping wet, to the door at the precise time when the minister was speaking to his wife of his trust in God. If he had come five minutes sooner or later he would not have heard what he did; and the family would not have received the help they needed.

These things did not come by chance. There is no such thing as chance, or luck. *God orders every thing.* God ordered this traveller to go on his journey. He ordered him when and where to go. He ordered the storm when to rise and when to burst. He ordered all things connected with it in such a way as to bring the stranger to the door at the very moment when this good man was telling of his simple trust in God. This clearly shows what pains, so to speak, God took in order to comfort His servant in that dark and trying hour. Just so a mother acts. She gives all she has; she does all she can to help and comfort her child. And this is what God means when He says,

" As one whom his mother comforteth, so will I comfort you."

In times of want, God is a wonderful Comforter.

But, thirdly, God is a wonderful Comforter IN TIMES OF SORROW.

This world is often called " a world of sorrow." It may well be called so, because there is much sorrow in it. When you kindle a fire you know how soon the sparks appear, and how they keep flying upwards as long as the fire burns. And the Bible tells us that it is as natural for people in this world to have sorrows as it is for sparks to appear while the fire is burning. When Jesus was on earth He was spoken of as "*a Man of sorrows.*" We cannot pass through this world without having sorrow. Some persons have more sorrow than others, but every one must have some. Listen to these four lines about sorrow. They were written by a good man many years ago. He had a great deal of sorrow himself, and what he says about sorrow in these lines is just as true as any thing in the Bible:—

"The path of sorrow, and that path *alone*,
   Leads to the land where sorrow is unknown;
   No trav'ler ever reached that blest abode
   Who found not thorns and briers on his road."

"Thorns and briers" here, mean troubles and trials, — the things that occasion us sorrow.

Many persons have sorrow in this world on account of the pain and suffering which sickness causes. Others have sorrow on account of the loss of their children or parents, their relatives or friends. Parents often have sorrow on account of the bad conduct of their children. Some persons have sorrow because they are so poor that they cannot get what they need; while others, again, have sorrow because they cannot keep what they have got. And we must all have our share of sorrow in one way or another. And if this is true, then it is very important that we should have a friend who can give us comfort when sorrow comes. And Jesus is just the Friend we need for this purpose. He is a wonderful Comforter in times of sorrow. If we are loving and serving Him, He says to each of us, "As one whom his mother comforteth, *so* will I comfort you."

Let me give you an example or two of the way in which Jesus comforts His people in times of sorrow.

THE BIBLE IN A COAL MINE.

In one of the coal mines of England, a youth, about fifteen years of age, was working by the side of his father, who was a pious man, and brought up his family, as the apostle says, "in the nurture and admonition of the Lord."

The father was in the habit of carrying with him a small pocket Bible; and the son, who had received one at the Sunday-school, followed the good example of his father in this matter. Thus he always had God's blessed Word with him, and whenever he had a little time to rest from his labor, he read it by the light of his lamp.

They were working together once in a newly-opened section of the mine, and the father had just stepped aside to get a particular tool that he wanted, when the arch above them suddenly fell down between him and his son. The father was greatly alarmed, for he supposed that his poor boy had instantly been crushed to death. He ran towards the place and called to his son, who presently answered his call from beneath a dense mass of earth and coal.

"My son," cried the father, "are you living?"

"Yes, father; but my legs are under a rock."

"Where is your lamp, my boy?"

"It is still burning, father."

"What are you doing, my dear son? and how do you feel?"

"I am reading my Bible, father, and the blessed Saviour is strengthening and comforting me."

These were the last words of that dear boy. For very soon his lamp went out, and he died for the want of fresh air, and went into the presence of that Saviour whom he loved.

It was a very sorrowful position in which this poor boy found himself, so suddenly and unexpectedly. His father or mother, his teacher or minister, could do nothing to comfort him then. But Jesus came near, in the darkness of the mine, as he lay crushed beneath the rock, and "as one whom his mother comforteth, so did He comfort him."

Here is an example of a little girl whom Jesus comforted in a time of sorrow. Her name was Nellie. In going along the street one day she met with a sad accident. Some foolish boys were amusing themselves with throwing stones. One of these struck Nellie on the eye, and hurt her very much. She was in such pain that she had to be carried home. Her father sent for the doctor. He carefully examined the wounded eye, and then said that she would have to undergo a very painful operation. When the time came for the operation she was sitting on her father's knee. He said to her, —

"Nellie, my dear, are you ready?"

"Not quite, father," she replied. "I should like to wait a minute; I have not yet prayed to God."

Then with her little hands folded together, she offered this simple prayer: —

"O Lord, forgive the little boy who hurt me, and help me to bear the pain well; and may Jesus be with me. Amen."

Then she said, "Father, I am ready now." And she bore the pain of the operation without a cry, so that all who were present looked on with surprise and astonishment at her great patience. But it was Jesus who was with her, and helped her to bear the pain so well. "As one whom his mother comforteth, so did He comfort her" in her time of sorrow.

Jesus is a wonderful Comforter in times when we most need comfort. These are *times of danger — times of want —* and *times of sorrow.*

And these are things we must all meet. But Jesus is the only one who can give us real comfort when we meet them. Unless we know Jesus, and make Him our friend, we shall be like the soldier who goes to battle without weapons; or like the sailor who goes to sea without an anchor. Let us give ourselves to Jesus, and love and serve Him now, and we shall find that He is a wonderful Comforter. And in all our times of danger, want, and sorrow, we shall hear Him say: "As one whom his mother comforteth, so will I comfort you."

III.

THE WONDERFUL GUIDE.

" I will guide thee with mine eye." — PSALM xxxii. 8.

IF we had to travel through a sandy desert or a vast wilderness, in which were no beaten paths, it would be most important for us to have a guide; or if we had to go through a dark cavern, like the Mammoth Cave of Kentucky, in which there were many winding paths and dangerous pitfalls, we should certainly lose our *way*, and very probably our *lives* also, unless we had a guide.

Now, the world in which we live may well be compared to a dark cavern, and we never can make our way safely through it unless we have a guide who can both point out the right path and also give us light that we may see how to walk in it.

But it is not only in dark caverns that guides are necessary. Often when travelling in the clear light of day we may lose our way if we venture without a guide.

I remember a case of this kind occurring when I was in Switzerland. We had made arrangements one evening to go on foot, the next day, across one of the Swiss mountains. While we were engaging our guide an English gentleman joined us. He was travelling alone, and intended to go over the same mountain the next morning. He inquired what was the charge for a guide; but thinking the terms too high, he said "he didn't care to take a guide; that he was not afraid, but believed he could find the way by himself." The next morning he started an hour or two before us. And when we were half way over, in one of the wildest parts of the mountain, where there was nothing that *we* could see to show the path, our guide stopped and pointed out a man who had missed the track, and wandered far, far away in the wrong direction. It proved to be the traveller who had been so sure he could find the way without help. Our guide said there was no outlet in the direction he was going; and that if he went on much further he would surely perish. Then, in his good nature, the guide climbed a high point on the side of the mountain, and cried out, with a voice like a trumpet, " Come back! come back!" The wanderer heard the friendly call. He retraced his steps and was saved.

Now, if we start in the journey of life without a guide we shall be sure to go astray, and wander from the right path.

We shall find many guides offering their services, but who will only lead us on to ruin. We are better without them. The only safe guide, on whom we may always rely with confidence, is Jesus, our Saviour. He offers Himself to us for this purpose. It is He who says, so tenderly, in the language of our text, " I will guide thee with mine eye."

What wonderful power there is in the eye! How much can be said through it, without opening the lips to speak! Love, hatred, pleasure, pain, joy, and sorrow, may all be expressed by looks as well as by words.

You remember the night in which Jesus was betrayed. After Peter had three times denied that he knew his Master, we read that "The Lord turned and — *looked* — on Peter." What meaning there was in that look!

It reminded Peter of the boasting promise he had so confidently made a little while before, when he solemnly declared his readiness to die for his Master, and his purpose never to leave Him, though all men should forsake Him. As the waters burst out from the rock in the wilderness, when smitten by the rod of Moses, so the tears of Peter's penitence gushed forth under the power of that look; and, as we read, "he went out and wept bitterly."

The words of this text set Jesus before us as — "*The Wonderful Guide.*"

Jesus has three things that He makes use of in guiding His people, and which show us what a wonderful Guide He is.

In the first place, He has A WONDERFUL EYE.

" I will guide thee with mine eye." The eye is the emblem of knowledge. And the Bible tells us that " the eye of the Lord is in every place, beholding the evil and the good."

This wonderful eye, that takes all things in, shows what perfect knowledge Jesus has for guiding His people.

It is important for a guide to have a clear and proper knowledge of every thing the persons he is guiding will need in their journey. Suppose you start on a journey. At night it becomes very cold; but your guide has provided no warm clothing, and made no preparations for a fire; then how much suffering there will be! or suppose there is a river to be crossed, and you have no means of crossing it, what trouble that will cause! or suppose that your journey is to last for several days, and your guide, not knowing that it is impossible to procure food on the way, neglects to take a full supply of such things as you will need, how much suffering must follow!

But if we take Jesus for our Guide, in the journey of life which is before us, we need fear none of these things. "He seeth the end from the beginning." He knows every thing that we can need through the whole course of our journey. His wonderful eye takes in, at a glance, the guidance which His people need, and He leads them in the right way.

Here is an example of the way in which He does this.

A young man had occasion to go to a distant city. The business which called him there was important. It was necessary, in order to accomplish it, that he should reach the end of his journey by a certain time. He was travelling alone, on horseback, through a wild part of the country that was very thinly settled. He had not clear directions respecting the road; and when he was half way through the journey, he unexpectedly found that the road forked into two branches, running in different directions. This was a difficulty for which he was not prepared. He looked around for some friendly house or hut, where he might learn which road to take. But there was none. For miles beyond he saw nothing but the deep, dark forest; and before him lay the two different roads. If he took the wrong one, or even if he returned to the nearest house to inquire, it would be too late to accomplish the business he had on hand. Here was a difficulty. What should he do? He had been taught by a Christian mother. He knew that God had promised to guide His people in every time of trouble. So he lifted up his heart in earnest prayer to God to show him the right way. And as his thoughts went up towards heaven, it was natural for him to look in the direction in which his thoughts were led. And as his eyes were thus lifted up he saw something half hidden by the leaves of the trees. When he had finished his prayer he drew near to examine the object which had attracted his attention. It proved to be a *guide-board!*

We can imagine his surprise and joy as he read there, in plain, bold letters, the direction which gave him the guidance he so much needed. It said to him, as plainly as a voice from heaven, "This is the way; walk thou in it." He remembered the promise in the Bible in which God says to His people: "Before they call, I will answer; and while they are yet speaking, I will hear." (Is. lxv. 24.) His heart overflowed with grateful love and wonder, to think how truly that sweet promise had been fulfilled in his case; and he went on his way rejoicing. He reached his destination in time to attend successfully to his business. Hitherto he had not been a decided Christian, but from that day he began to love and serve God.

Here we see how, with His wonderful eye, Jesus guided this young man when he knew not which way to go. He looked up to Him for direction, and he found it. Jesus is a wonderful Guide. The first thing which He has in guiding His people is a wonderful eye.

The second thing which Jesus has in guiding His people is A WONDERFUL HAND.

Now, as the eye represents knowledge so the hand represents power. And it is because Jesus has a wonderful eye to see what His people need, and a wonderful hand to enable Him to supply their need, that He is such a wonderful Guide. He makes use of His eye and His hand, His knowledge and His power, to guide and help His people. Let me show you how He does this.

Many years ago, Admiral Williams was crossing the Atlantic Ocean in command of a frigate belonging to the English navy. The course he was sailing brought him within sight of the Island of Ascension. This is a small, barren island, about eight miles in length and six in breadth, lying between Africa and Brazil. Until the Emperor Napoleon Bonaparte was imprisoned on the Island of St. Helena, this island was uninhabited. Then the English government built a fort on it, and the soldiers cultivated it. But the time to which our story refers was before this. No one lived on the island then, and ships never stopped there, unless they wanted to get a supply of turtles, as they were always to be found along the shores in great numbers.

But the admiral was not in want of turtles for his crew. Yet no sooner did the island, in the far distance, appear in sight, than a strange desire came over him to go out of his course, and steer towards it.

He felt sure if he did so, that his officers and crew would think it very strange, as he could give no reason for changing the ship's course. He tried to throw off this feeling, but could not do it. The desire grew stronger and stronger, and at last he made up his mind to follow this strange impression, and see to what it would lead.

Calling his lieutenant, he ordered him to get ready to put the ship about, and steer for the Island of Ascension. The officer ventured respectfully to suggest to the admiral how much this would delay them, and to ask what would be gained by this change of course. The admiral said he could not tell, but that he felt a strong desire to go.

"Sir," said the lieutenant, "the men are just going to dinner; shall the order be delayed till they get through?"

Without further reply, the admiral himself gave the order, which is never disobeyed on ship-board: "Ready, about!"

At once the men sprang to their

THE WONDERFUL GUIDE.

stations. The vessel was put about; and directly was making her way towards the distant island.

All on board wondered what this meant, and why the ship was changing her course to visit an uninhabited island. As they drew near all were on the lookout, and every eye was eagerly turned towards the island. Soon those who had the best glasses were greatly excited about an object on shore, which at first they could not make out. "It's something white," said one. "It's a flag; it's a signal," said another. It was a signal of distress, and they soon saw men upon the island.

When they came near, the ship "hove to," and a boat was sent ashore. In a little while the boat returned, bringing with her sixteen men who had been cast ashore on that island some days before. The want of food had caused them extreme suffering; and knowing that the island was rarely visited by passing vessels, they had done all that could be done in setting up their signal on the highest point of the coast, and praying earnestly that God would send them relief. Solomon tells us that "the heart of a king is in the hand of the Lord, and He turneth whithersoever He will, as the rivers of water are turned." And we have a beautiful illustration of this truth, when we see how God's hand turned the heart of this good sailor to do what He wished to have done. And it is because God has power over the hearts of all men, that He can use His wonderful hand to guide His people in all their ways.

The second thing that Jesus has to help Him in guiding His people is *a wonderful hand.*

The third thing that He has to help Him in guiding His people is A WONDERFUL BOOK.

When we travel through foreign countries we always need a guide-book. This book will tell us the distances from one place to another; the best roads, the best places at which to stop, and all we need to know, in order to make the journey both safe and comfortable.

And Jesus has such a book for the use of those who wish to be guided through this world, and brought safe to heaven at last. The Bible is this book. It is a wonderful book for many reasons; and of these the chief is its wonderful power to guide lost sinners to Jesus. Let me give you one or two illustrations to show how wonderful the Bible is in its guiding power.

A few years since there was a terrible war in India. It was caused by the mutiny or rebellion of the native troops belonging to the English government. A Christian lady, living in India, spent much of her time in visiting the sick and wounded soldiers in one of the hospitals. One day, while reading to the sick men, she was interrupted by some Scotch soldiers coming in to say good-by to their wounded and suffering comrades. Before they left she spoke a few kind and solemn words to them, reminding them of the danger to which they would be exposed, and the importance of being always prepared to die. Then she read to them the twenty-third psalm, and commended them to God in prayer. As they shook hands with her in parting, the soldiers, one by one, asked for a little book, or tract. Opening her satchel, she gave one to each. But just as she reached the last of them her supply failed and she had none to give him. He begged so earnestly for a parting token, that, taking a blank leaf of paper from one of her books, she wrote upon it several texts of Scripture, with a verse or two of the hymn beginning, —

"How sweet the name of Jesus sounds,
In a believer's ear."

Handing him this leaf, she said she hoped to meet him in heaven.

Many months passed away. During this time the regiment to which those men belonged had marched a long way up into the country, for the relief of the city of Lucknow, which had been besieged by the native troops. This regiment had passed through many hard-fought battles, besides the fatigues and exposures of long marches in a hot climate.

One day, while the same lady was

going through the hospital, she was told that a sick soldier, just brought in, wished to see her. She went to his cot, and found a man whom she did not recognize.

He looked earnestly at her and said, —

"You don't know me, madam, but I've heard a great deal about you." As he spoke, he took from his bosom a piece of paper stained with blood, and showed her the texts she had written upon it for a soldier, some months before.

"That soldier," said he, "was my companion in the march from Cawnpoore to Lucknow. Often, when we halted in our march, he would take this leaf, and read and ponder over it. He learned these words by heart, and they guided him to Jesus. In one of the dreadful battles before Lucknow, a ball struck him, and he fell. We carried him from the field to the surgeon; but it was too late. His life was ebbing fast away. 'Well, James,' he said to me, 'I'm going home first. We have often talked together about that blessed home. Don't be sorry for me. I'm happy. I feel the truth of the hymn that Christian lady wrote for me,—

"How sweet the name of Jesus sounds."

Read me the precious words once

more before I go.' I took from his bosom this leaf, now wet with his blood, and read: 'We know that if our earthly house of this tabernacle be dissolved, we have a building of God, a house not made with hands, eternal in the heavens.' 'For the love of Christ constraineth us.' 'Yes,' said he, 'the love of Christ constraineth us. I'm almost home. I'll be there to welcome you. Good-by, my dear fel—' The word died upon his lips, and he was gone. I knelt down by his side, and took this torn and blood-stained leaf from his dead hand, and put it in my own bosom. Then we buried him.

Since then I have encountered many hardships and dangers, and now am here to die. And so, ma'am, you'll please forgive me for making so bold as to speak to you. I wanted before I die to thank you for giving this leaf to my comrade. It guided him to Jesus, and he guided me."

Quite overcome by her feelings, the lady was unable to speak. She could only press the dying soldier's hand as her tears fell fast upon his pillow. He died soon after, and joined his comrade in that bright and happy world, "where the wicked cease from troubling, and the weary are at rest."

Here we see what a wonderful book the Bible is for guiding lost souls to Jesus.

Now let me give you my last illustration about this wonderful book.

In a village in the north of England there lived, some years ago, a widow with six children, all of whom were Sabbath school scholars. Their father was an officer in the British navy when he died, leaving his wife with the care of this large family. The bad conduct of the eldest son proved a great trial to his mother, whom he refused to obey. His companions were the worst boys in the village; and after his father's death he became more disobedient than ever. His sad mother wept and prayed over him, but he went on in his wickedness. Finding that she could not control him, she concluded to send him to sea, hoping the strict discipline on shipboard might have a good effect on him. When packing his chest, his mother slipped in a pocket Bible, lifting up her heart in prayer that God would bless it to him, and make it the means of changing his heart, and saving his soul. He went very far astray; but his mother's prayers followed him wherever he went.

He seldom wrote to his mother, and never came back to her. She wept and mourned, but still hoped on that God would finally save him. At last the sad tidings came that the vessel in which he sailed had been lost at sea. Then his mother's heart was filled with sorrow; but her greatest grief was that she could not learn if he had repented of his sins and become a Christian before he died. To have known this would have been the sweetest comfort to her.

One stormy night in winter, long after this, while she and her children were sitting by their cheerful fireside, a knock was heard at the door. On opening it, they found there a weary, weather-beaten sailor. He said he was cold and hungry, and begged for food and shelter. They asked him in; for, since her son had gone to sea, the mother always felt her heart drawn towards sailors when in trouble. She thought of her own dear boy, and tried to be as kind to a poor sailor as she would wish others to be to her son, should he be in want.

So they welcomed the sailor, and gave him a seat by the fire, while supper was preparing for him. As he warmed himself, they asked about his voyages, the various countries he had visited, and the different vessels he had sailed in. He answered their questions freely, telling them all about his sufferings and dangers, and speaking particularly of a voyage in which he had been wrecked.

"We were overtaken by a violent tempest," said he, "and our ship was driven ashore, and dashed to pieces. All the crew were lost but myself and one companion. We were thrown upon the beach, where my shipmate soon died, leaving me alone. He had once been the terror of the ship for his profanity and ungodliness. But a wonderful change had taken place in him, and for some time before his death he had been a Bible-reading, praying Christian, an example to all on board for his piety.

"While lying on the beach, just before he died, he drew a Bible from his bosom and pressed it to his lips. Then he handed it to me, and said, 'Bob, this book has been the best friend I ever had. You know how different I have been lately from what I used to be. I owe it all to this book. I found it one day in overhauling my chest. On opening it, I saw my name written by my mother. It brought up afresh the thought of her tender love, and her earnest prayers for me. It reminded me of my happy home, when a boy, in dear old England. I resolved to read it. I did so. It showed me what a sinner I was. It led me to Jesus. In Him I found a Saviour. I'm going to Him now. I shan't need this blessed book any more, so now I give it to you, Bob. Read it. Pray over it, and it will save your soul, as it has saved mine.'

"Then, as he said this, he fell back upon the sand and died, with a prayer to Jesus on his lips."

"'Have you that Bible with you?" asked the agitated mother.

"Oh, yes! ma'am, I've never parted with it since that day," said he, carefully taking it from his bosom, and handing it to her.

Tremblingly she seized it, and turning to the blank page she saw in her own handwriting the name of her dear lost boy.

"'Tis his! 'tis his! My son! my son! saved at last!" she exclaimed, and burst into tears of joy and thankfulness. Her prayers had been answered; and this wonderful book, the Bible, had been made use of to guide that poor wayward, wandering son to Jesus, and to heaven.

Jesus is a wonderful Guide.

There are three things He makes use of in guiding His people which show this. The first of these is *a wonderful eye;* the second is *a wonderful hand;* the third is *a wonderful book.*

My dear children, will you not all make up your minds to take Jesus as your Guide? This is what He desires you to do when He says, "Wilt thou not, from this time, cry unto me, *My Father, Thou art the Guide of my youth?*" (Jer. iii. 4.) If we take Jesus for our Guide, and *follow* His guidance, we shall most surely find Him to be a wonderful Guide. He will lead us safely through this wicked world, and bring us home to Himself in heaven. Let the prayer go up from every heart, —

> "Guide me, O Thou gracious Saviour,
>   Pilgrim through this foreign land:
> I am weak, but Thou art mighty,
>   Hold me with Thy powerful hand."

Cambridge: Press of John Wilson and Son.

Any book on this list sent by mail, postage prepaid, on receipt of the Price.

530 Broadway, New York,
March, 1874.

ROBERT CARTER & BROTHERS'
NEW BOOKS.

THE AUTOBIOGRAPHY OF THOMAS GUTHRIE, D.D.
And Memoir by his Sons. Vol. I. $2.00.

"It is told in the chattiest, simplest, most unaffected way imaginable, and the pages are full of quaint, racy anecdotes, recounted in the most characteristic manner." — *London Daily News.*

New uniform Edition of the
WORKS OF THOMAS GUTHRIE, D.D.
In 9 volumes. 12mo. (The volumes are sold separately.) $13.50.

Memorial Volume.
SERMONS BY THE LATE ROBERT S. CANDLISH, D.D.
With a Biographical Preface. $2.00.

THE ARGUMENT OF THE BOOK OF JOB UNFOLDED.
By the Rev. W. H. Green, D.D., of Princeton Theological Seminary. 12mo. $1.75.

SONGS OF THE SOUL,
   Gathered out of many Lands and Ages. By S. I. Prime, D.D. $5.00.

   By the Author of the "Wide Wide World."
THE LITTLE CAMP ON EAGLE HILL. $1.25.

WILLOW BROOK. $1.25.

   By the Author of "Win and Wear."
MABEL HAZARD'S THOROUGHFARE. $1.25.

DOORS OUTWARD:
   A Tale. $1.25.

   By the Rev. Dr. Macduff.
THE HEALING WATERS OF ISRAEL. $1.25.

THE GATES OF PRAYER.
   A Book of Private Devotion for Morning and Evening $1.00.

NOTES ON EXODUS.
   Vol. I   From Egypt to Sinai.   By M. W. Jacobus, D.D $1.00.

ROCKBOURNE:
   A Tale. By Marion Eliza Weir. $1.25.

LITTLE TRIX;
   or, Grandma's Lessons. $0.60.

MAGGIE'S MISTAKE:
   A School Girl's Story. With 18 Illustrations. $1.25.

BETWEEN THE CLIFFS.
   By Emma Marshall. And "Wandering May." In one volume. $1.00.

DARE TO DO RIGHT SERIES.
By Julia A. Mathews. Containing "Grandfather's Faith," "Our Four Boys," "Giuseppe's Home," "Nellie's Stumbling-Block," and "Susy's Sacrifice." 5 vols. In a box. $5.50.

GIUSEPPE'S HOME (new).
Separate. $1.10.

MISS ASHTON'S GIRLS. By Joanna H. Mathews :—
1. FANNY'S BIRTHDAY GIFT $1.25
2. THE NEW SCHOLARS 1.25
(other volumes preparing.)

SILVER KEYS: By A. L. O. E.
A Tale. $0.75.

*CARTERS' CHEAP SABBATH SCHOOL LIBRARY.
50 vols. In neat cloth. In a wooden case. Net $20.00.

LEAVES FROM THE TREE OF LIFE.
By Richard Newton, D.D. 16mo. $1.25.

HARRY AND DOLLY LIBRARY.
By the Author of "Little Kitty's Library." 6 vols. $3.00.

FUN AND WORK.
By the Author of "Little Kitty's Library." $0.50.

TRUFFLE NEPHEWS.
And their New Charity. By the Rev. P. B. Power. $1.00.

SHE SPAKE OF HIM.
A Memoria. of Mrs. Dening. By Mrs. Guinness. $1.25

THE REEF.
And other Parables. By the Rev. E. H. Bickersteth. 16mo. Illustrated. $1.25.

YESTERDAY, TO-DAY, AND FOREVER.
By Bickersteth. Cheap Edition. $1.25.

RYLE'S NOTES ON THE GOSPELS.
  now complete in 7 volumes. $10.50. (Containing Matthew, 1 vol.; Mark, 1 vol.; Luke, 2 vols.; and John, 3 vols. All the volumes sold separately at $1 50 per vol.)

*HENRY'S COMMENTARY ON THE BIBLE.
  New Edition. In 9 vols. cloth, $27.00; or in 5 vols. quarto sheep, $25.00.

THE CHURCH IN THE HOUSE.
  Lessons on the Acts of the Apostles. By the Rev. WILLIAM ARNOT. $2.50.

THIS PRESENT WORLD.
  By the Same. $1.25.

SERMONS AND LECTURES.
  From the unpublished manuscripts of the late JAMES HAMILTON, D.D. $2.50.

SYNOPTICAL LECTURES ON THE BIBLE.
  From Genesis to Song of Solomon. By the Rev. DONALD FRASER. $2.00.

THE WORD OF LIFE.
  By CHARLES J. BROWN, D.D. 12mo. $1.50.

THE CHRIST OF GOD.
  By the Rev. HORATIUS BONAR, D.D. $1.25.

THE RELATIONS OF THE KINGDOM TO THE WORLD.
  By Dr. DYKES. $1.25.

BLENDING LIGHTS;
  or, The Relations of Natural Science, Archæology, and History, to the Bible. By WILLIAM FRASER, LL.D. $2.00.

A LAWYER ABROAD.
  What to See and How to See. By HENRY DAY.

THE RESURRECTION OF THE DEAD.
By the Rev. William Hanna, D.D. 12mo.

THE LAWS OF THE KINGDOM.
By the Rev. J. Oswald Dykes. $1.25.

PISGAH VIEWS;
Or, The Negative Attractions of Heaven. By Octavius Winslow, D.D. $1.25.

COMFORT YE, COMFORT YE.
Being God's Word of Comfort addressed to his Church in the last twenty-seven chapters of Isaiah. By J. R. Macduff, D.D. $1.50.

"Dr. Macduff has a rare and happy faculty for investing the different portions of the Bible with freshness and force and living interest. He blends happily the critical intellect of the student and the fervid heart of the devout Christian. This latest of his works seems to us in many respects his choicest and best." — *Star*.

THE EVERLASTING RIGHTEOUSNESS;
Or, How shall Man be Just with God. By Horatius Bonar, D.D. $1.25.

THE WONDERFUL LAMP,
And other Addresses to Children. By A. MacLeod, D.D. $1.00.

"Dr. MacLeod understands children. There seems to be a clear intellectual apprehension of their wants and of the way in which they are to be met: but th best part of his power of ministration comes from his vital sympathy with youn natures."

SCRIPTURE ITSELF THE ILLUSTRATOR.
By the Rev. G. S. Bowes. $1.50.

THE CULTURE OF PLEASURE;
Or, The Enjoyment of Life in its Social and Religious Aspects. By the author of the "Mirage of Life." 12mo, gilt top. $2.00.

OLIVER CROMWELL.
By J. H. Merle D'Aubigné, D.D. 12mo. New edition. $1.25.

HYMNS OF THE CHURCH MILITANT.
By Miss Anna Warner. New edition. 16mo. $1.50.

ABLE TO SAVE.
By the author of "Pathway of Promise." New edition. 16mo. $1.00.

NOT BREAD ALONE;
Or, Miss Helen's Neighbors By Jennie M. Drinkwater. $1.25.

MORAG:
A Tale of the Highlands of Scotland. $1.25

RHODA'S CORNER.
By Annie M. Mitchell Payne. $1.25.

BRIGHTSIDE.
By Mrs. E. Bedell Benjamin. 16mo. $1.25.

AUNT SAIDEE'S COW.
By Miss S. J. Prichard. $1.25.

FAITHFUL IN LITTLE;
Or, The Story of a Carrier Dove By the author of "Daisy Maynard." $1.00.

By JOANNA H. MATHEWS.

THE KITTY AND LULU BOOKS. 6 vols.	$6.00
THE BESSIE BOOKS. 6 vols.	7.50
THE FLOWERETS. 6 vols.	3.60
LITTLE SUNBEAMS. 6 vols.	6.00

"The child-world we are here introduced to is delightfully real. The children talk and act so naturally that we feel real live children must have sat for their portraits." — *Baltimore Christian Advocate.*

"We can wish our young readers no greater pleasure than an acquaintance with dear, cute little Bessie and her companions, old and young, brute and human.' —*American Presbyterian.*

By EMILY SARAH HOLT.

ISOULT BARRY OF WYSNCOTE	$1.50
ROBIN TREMAYNE: A TALE	1.50
ASHCLIFFE HALL: A TALE	1.25
THE WELL IN THE DESERT	1.25

"Whether it is regarded in its historical or its religious aspect, 'Isoult Barry of Wynscote' is the finest contribution to English literature of its peculiar class which has been made in the present century." — *American Baptist.*

By the Author of the "Wide Wide World."

A STORY OF SMALL BEGINNINGS.

CONTAINING

WHAT SHE COULD.	HOUSE IN TOWN.
OPPORTUNITIES.	TRADING.

4 volumes. In a box $5.00

"As a writer of fresh, bright, and, above all, natural religious stories, we believe Miss Warner has no superior." — *Echo.*

"Miss Warner's little girls are always Bible readers and thinkers. Surrounded by untoward influences, they are led by the Spirit on to victory Their characters are charming." — *Baptist Union.*

Had You Been in His Place.
A powerful and admirable Temperance Story. By Lizzie Bates. 16mo. $1.25.

The Curate's Home.
By Agnes Giberne, author of "Aimee," &c. $1.25.

By the same Author.

Aimée.
A Tale of the Days of James the Second. 12mo. $1.50

The Day Star;
Or, The Gospel Story for the Little Ones. 16 tinted illustrations. $1.25.

Who Won.
By the author of "Win and Wear." 16mo. $1.25.

By the same Author.

WIN AND WEAR SERIES. 6 vols.	$7.50
THE LEDGESIDE SERIES. 6 vols.	7.50
THE GREEN MOUNTAIN STORIES. 5 vols.	6.00
BUTTERFLY'S FLIGHTS. 3 vols.	2.25

Only Ned;
Or, Grandma's Message. By Jennie M. Drinkwater 16mo. $1 25.

The Warrior Judges.
By the Rev. Dr. Macduff. 16mo. 3 illustrations. $1.00

The Beatitudes of the Kingdom.
By the Rev. J. Oswald Dykes. 16mo. $1.25.

The Kings of Israel and Judah.
Their History explained to Children. By the author of the "Peep of Day." 27 illustrations. $1.50.

"We commend every parent and every Sunday-school teacher in the land to get a copy. It is needless to speak of the delightful way in which the author treats the subject." — *S. S. Times*

Thought-Hives.

(Third Thousand.) By the Rev. T. L. CUYLER, author of 'The Empty Crib," "Cedar Christian," &c. Portrait by Ritchie. $1.75.

" Dr. Cuyler crowds many thoughts into few words. He makes dry bones ive; his words are sermons, his sentences shafts of light." — *Baptist Union.*

The Song of the New Creation,

And Other Pieces. By Horatius Bonar, D.D. 16mo. $1.25.

" All the sweetest characteristics of Dr. Bonar's previous volumes of sacred poetry are reproduced in this new collection. No hymn-writer of this century has surpassed him in rendering the spirit and life of the Word of God into verse." — *Christian Intelligencer*

The Wars of the Huguenots.

By the Rev. Dr. Hanna. 16mo. $1.25.

Saint Paul in Rome;

Or, The Teachings, Fellowships, and Dying Testimony of the Great Apostle in the City of the Cæsars. By J. R. Macduff, D.D. 16mo. $1.25.

Jacobus' Commentaries.

New Editions, at reduced prices.

GENESIS. 2 vols in one	$1.50
MATTHEW AND MARK	1.50
LUKE AND JOHN	1.50
ACTS	1.50
* Question Books adapted to each. Per dozen	1.80

The Scots Worthies.

By John Howie. With more than 100 illustrations. Tirted paper, gilt edges. $3.50.

Christianity and Positivism.

A Series of Lectures by Dr. McCosh. Fifth thousand $1.75.

Tales of Christian Life.
By the author of the "Schönberg-Cotta Family.' 5 vols. In box. $5.00.

CRIPPLE OF ANTIOCH.	TWO VOCATIONS.
MARTYRS OF SPAIN.	TALES AND SKETCHES.

WANDERINGS OVER BIBLE LANDS.

"This new and tasteful edition of these charming books, as good as they are delightful, will make them more than ever popular." — *Advance.*

Nature's Wonders.
By the Rev. Dr. Newton, author of "Bible Wonders," "Great Pilot," "Safe Compass," &c. 16mo. $1.25.

By the same Author.

THE JEWEL CASE. 6 vols.	$7.50
BIBLE WONDERS	1.25
RILLS FROM THE FOUNTAIN	1.25
JEWISH TABERNACLE	1.25

Dr. Chalmers' Sermons.
Cheap Edition. 2 volumes in 1. 1105 double column pages. Price reduced to $3.00.

Charnock on the Attributes.
New and Cheap Edition. 2 volumes in 1; containing 1149 large 8vo pages. Price reduced to $3.00.

McCheyne's Works.
Cheap and Neat Edition. Comprising his Life, Letters, Lectures, and Sermons 2 volumes in 1. 1074 pages. 8vo Price reduced to $3.00.

Family Worship.
A series of Prayers for Morning and Evening throughout the year. New Edition, at half the former price. $2.50.

Life of Christ.
By William Hanna, D.D 3 vols. 12mo $4.50.

www.ingramcontent.com/pod-product-compliance
Lightning Source LLC
Chambersburg PA
CBHW031854220426
43663CB00006B/616